To: _____

From: _____

Date: _____

Occasion: _____

Special Thoughts

_____

_____

_____

_____

_____

_____

_____

There's
MAGIC
in
DISCOVERY

by

John J. Pelizza, Ph.D.

Published by:
Pelizza & Associates
P.O. Box 225
North Chatham, New York 12132

Edited by: Phillip Niles

Cover & Text Design by: Bonnie S. Pelizza

Illustrations by: Kimberly P. Hart

Published by Pelizza & Associates, P.O. Box 225, North Chatham, New York 12132, (518) 766-4849.

Printed and bound in the United States of America.
ISBN 0-9614872-2-4

DEDICATION

Twenty-five years ago on a blind date, I made my "greatest discovery", I met my wife, Bonnie. During our years together, she taught me to "dream" and to take action so that I could grow and "discover". She is the "special person" in my life who makes each day *BETTER --- GOOD --- TERRIFIC*. To her I lovingly dedicate this book.

Table of Contents

v

FOREWORD

Before we start, let's talk about a concept that appears frequently in this book. You'll see the words **_BETTER -- GOOD_** a lot in these pages.

What do they mean?

We all know what it means to feel GOOD, but for many people GOOD isn't part of their reality anymore. Some people are hurting so bad, GOOD no longer exists for them. That's sad, but that's the way it is.

Everyone understands BETTER, though. You have to be BETTER before you can get to GOOD.

Let me give you an example: My kids and I live in different worlds, in many ways. If something's not going right with my kids, and I tell them, "We can make this GOOD," they'll probably tune me right out. But if I say, "Well, let's see if we can make this BETTER," that connects. "GOOD" sounds suspicious, but they understand "BETTER."

You have to be BETTER
before you can get to GOOD

vii

BETTER makes sense, right? Here's another illustration: Recently I did a presentation for one of the major banks in New York City. I was there overnight, and they put me up at a midtown hotel.

I had a room on the tenth floor or so, and as I was looking out the window I saw a homeless person lying in an alley down below covered by a newspaper. If you've been to New York City in the last few years, you know what I'm talking about. Homeless people like this are an all too common sight.

Anyway, I thought about why I was in New York, and I thought about the person lying in the alley, and I wondered what would happen if I took the elevator down to the hotel lobby, walked out to the alley, leaned over this homeless person and said, "Hey, buddy, I've got some ideas that will make you feel GOOD!"

Can you imagine the reaction of this unfortunate fellow huddled under a newspaper in a New York City alley to my promises of feeling GOOD? "Get out of here, you crazy person!" is probably close to what would happen in that situation.

BETTER makes BETTER sense

And a lot of people are in the same boat --
and not just people like the homeless, either.
Many people are so far down that GOOD isn't even
in their reality anymore. You may have been there
once or twice in your life yourself.

But . . .

No matter how BAD someone's situation
might be, ask that person if it's possible they can
feel BETTER, and it's hard to imagine anyone
saying that it couldn't happen.

You may have had a lousy day at work, but
once you get home you can feel BETTER, right?

You may have had a fight yesterday with
someone close to you, but you can feel BETTER,
right?

Your boss may have called you in to tell you
that your performance on your job isn't where it
needs to be, but you can feel BETTER, right?

You may have just learned that the tax
refund you've been planning to use for that big
vacation isn't as big as you thought it would be,
but you can still feel BETTER, right?

You can still feel BETTER

In all of these situations, feeling GOOD is probably out of the question, but feeling BETTER is possible.

BETTER makes sense.

BETTER is achievable.

BETTER works.

And that's why this book always talks about BETTER -- GOOD, rather than simply GOOD.

The purpose of this book is to help you feel BETTER and do BETTER than you're doing now. You might be doing TERRIFIC already, or you might be doing TERRIBLE, but no matter what your situation you can still feel BETTER and do BETTER, right?

RIGHT!

So let's go!!

If you learn the concepts in this book and apply them in your daily life, you'll feel BETTER and do BETTER.

BETTER is achievable
IT WORKS

It has to happen!

Why?

Because you'll be doing things that will increase your ENERGY.

You'll be in the process of DISCOVERY.

You'll experience ACCOMPLISHMENT.

You'll be TAKING ACTION.

You'll have more ENERGY and feel **BETTER** more of the time, **GOOD** much of the time and **TERRIFIC** some of the time!!!

Now that you know what BETTER -- GOOD is all about, it's time to start exploring the MAGIC of DISCOVERY.

I hope you enjoy this book, and that it helps make BETTER -- GOOD a bigger part of the life you lead every single day.

More ENERGY means
you'll feel BETTER -- GOOD
more of the time

INTRODUCTION

INTRODUCTION

Is this you?

Tell the truth, now.

On Monday, you get up. You go to work. You come home, eat dinner, watch a little TV, and go to bed.

On Tuesday, you get up. You go to work. You come home, eat dinner, watch a little TV, then go to bed.

On Wednesday, you get up . . .

Got the idea?   Sound familiar?

Every day you do the same things, go to the same places, see the same old people with the same old attitudes.

By Tuesday you're bored.

By Wednesday you're tired.

By Thursday you're running on empty.

And by Friday you're exhausted.

As the week has gone on, you've lost more and more ENERGY. You need a weekend to recharge yourself just enough to start all over again on Monday.

It's sad.

Sad -- and a little bit sick.

Yet how many of us settle for living just like this?

Does it always have to be this way?

Is this "life"?

Do the rules say we **have** to live like this?

No.

Not at all.

You **DON'T** have to live like this.

It's your **CHOICE**.

Instead of dragging through your days and weeks, you can have abundant ENERGY. ENERGY to help you feel BETTER, live longer, do more, and to accomplish things you never thought possible.

How?

Through the **MAGIC OF DISCOVERY**, that's how!

Let's begin with a question: What would you like to do with the rest of your life? What would you like to do before you check out and die that would get you really EXCITED!

Have a pen or pencil handy? GOOD!

Get ready to make a list of what you'd like to do between now and checkout time that would get you REALLY EXCITED.

What's EXCITED?

EXCITED is a ten-year-old boy who loves fishing. His father has just told the boy that he's taking him away on a three-day fishing trip THIS weekend! *That's EXCITED!*

EXCITED is a woman who gets a small package from her boyfriend. She opens it, and inside finds a diamond engagement ring! *That's EXCITED!!*

EXCITED is a golfer whose shot on the third hole bounces right into the cup for a hole-in-one! *That's EXCITED!!!*

EXCITED is a high school senior who opens a formal-looking letter and finds out he or she's been accepted to one of the best colleges in the country! *That's EXCITED!!!!*

EXCITED is a company supervisor who delegates a difficult task to a new employee, and the employee gets it right the very first time! *That's EXCITED!!!!!*

EXCITED is a worker who receives an extremely challenging new task from his supervisor, and gets it right the very first time! *That's EXCITED!!!!!!*

Know what kind of EXCITED we're talking about? OK.

You give it a try.

THAT'S EXCITED!!!!

THAT'S EXCITED!!!!

What could happen in your life that would get you EXCITED like this -- *REALLY EXCITED?*

MAKE A LIST IN THE SPACES PROVIDED:

1. _____

_____

2. _____

_____

3. _____

_____

4. _____

_____

5. _____

_____

How did it go?

Were you SPECIFIC?

If you wrote "TRAVEL", did you say where?

If you said you'd like to be "FINANCIALLY INDEPENDENT", did you say how much money you want and what time frame you want it in?

If you wrote "BECOME FAMOUS", did you say how famous? By doing what?

If you put "CHANGE CAREERS", did you say into what?

Because it probably won't happen unless you're SPECIFIC about what will get you EXCITED.

Couldn't think of anything? No problem.

That's what this book is all about -- *DISCOVERY*.

This book will help you find ways -- simple ways -- to use *DISCOVERY* to create more ENERGY -- to help you feel *BETTER* every day of your life.

But the ultimate *DISCOVERY* you can achieve with the aid of this book is to find out what you really want from life -- what you *REALLY* want to do.

Because if every day seems the same, if you lose ENERGY as the week drags on, if your job doesn't "do it" for you, then you need to DISCOVER what it is that *will* do it for you -- what *will* get you EXCITED!

Once you make this key DISCOVERY, your mind will create the ENERGY needed to figure out how to get you to whatever it is that'll get you EXCITED -- not just once in a while, but every day!

You'll be living life at a HIGHER ENERGY LEVEL than you ever thought possible, doing the things that EXCITE you every day of your life.

It *can* happen because . . .

There's *MAGIC IN DISCOVERY!*

Ready to learn how?

All right!

Turn the page, and let's get started!!

PART I

POSITIVE DISCOVERY

N R E G Y E

Can you unscramble this word?

Give it a try!

Need a hint?

Think "power".

Another hint?

How about "electricity"?

Got it now?

SURE -- it's *ENERGY!*

What did you *feel* at the instant you knew what this word was?   A little surge of *ENERGY, right?*

This is a small example of a big idea.   It's called the *process of DISCOVERY.*   You discovered what the word was and your body instantly created a small *Surge of Energy*. And how did you *feel* at precisely that moment? *BETTER!!!*

POSITIVE DISCOVERY
creates ENERGY!

This principle, the **PRINCIPLE OF DISCOVERY,** is extremely simple: When you DISCOVER something POSITIVE in life, you feel **BETTER!!!**

You don't have to think about it -- it just happens. You have a **POSITIVE DISCOVERY,** your body creates **ENERGY,** you feel **BETTER!!!**

Now imagine that you're playing golf. It hasn't been a great round so far. A couple in the trees, a few short putts missed, a lot over par.

On the 17th green, you have a treacherous, twisting, downhill 50-foot putt.

You estimate the break and give the ball a firm yet careful rap. It winds down toward the hole, breaking first left, then right, then back a little to the left. It approaches the cup, hangs on the left lip for an agonizing instant, then drops!

You've had a **POSITIVE DISCOVERY,** and your body is flowing with **ENERGY.** You may jump in the air, toss your putter, or high-five your playing partners. You feel **BETTER -- GOOD,** despite your poor round, and you're flowing with **ENERGY.**

POSITIVE DISCOVERY
makes you feel BETTER!

In fact, if the putt was for something BIG, you might even feel *TERRIFIC* from your *POSITIVE DISCOVERY*. When this happened to golf pro Hale Irwin, who sunk such a putt on the 18th hole at the U.S. Open in 1990, the *ENERGY* he experienced made him feel *TERRIFIC*. He ran all the way around the green, high-fiving the entire gallery in a display of *ENERGY* never before witnessed in a major professional golf tournament -- *ENERGY* which helped propel Irwin all the way through a 19-hole playoff to victory!

Another example: Imagine you're driving through an unfamiliar countryside. The road bends to the left, and SUDDENLY, there it is. The most *beautiful view* you've ever seen. A range of stunning mountains fringed with puffy clouds turning golden in the rays of a rising sun. A dreamy valley, with a placid, misty river meandering through stately rows of graceful trees.

It's the most breathtaking view you've ever seen. You stop your car, and admire in wonder! You've **DISCOVERED** something wonderful.

How do you feel? Immediately you feel **BETTER**! You probably feel better than that. You feel **GOOD**! You may even feel **TERRIFIC!**

All this because you experienced a **POSITIVE DISCOVERY**.

PRINCIPLE OF + DISCOVERY

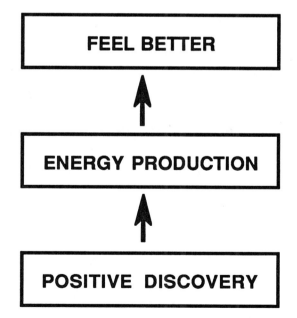

Why do children have so much *ENERGY*? Kids are constantly in the process of POSITIVE *DISCOVERY*. Each day brings them new experiences, new sights, new places, new learning.

Even the simplest things -- Grandma's big nose, Grandpa's bald head -- give kids a sense of *DISCOVERY* -- of new *ENERGY*.

Have you ever said to yourself, "If I only had *half the energy* my kids have."? Sure, you have. And you can --- and maybe more --- if you make *POSITIVE DISCOVERY* a part of your everyday life.

Think back to the last time you planned a big vacation -- a trip to someplace really special. What did you *feel* in the days, weeks, and months before that vacation every time you thought about it? Remember the excitement, the *ENERGY*? Remember how excited you got every time you talked about that vacation before you went?

We all need more ENERGY to feel BETTER

Before that vacation you were in a constant state of *POSITIVE DISCOVERY* -- thinking about new experiences, new sights, new surprises. So powerful were your thoughts about the *POSITIVE DISCOVERIES* that would occur on your trip that the *ENERGY* spilled over into the days and weeks even before you went!!

As adults, though, we're not on vacation every day. Too bad, you say! Maybe, but you can still enjoy the kind of ENERGY which *DISCOVERY* creates every day of your life -- *ENERGY* which can help you feel *BETTER* and do more.

You experience *POSITIVE DISCOVERY* in many ways.

*   When you hear a new song on the radio
*   When you find something you'd thought you'd lost
*   When you find a new restaurant you like
*   When you get a raise
*   When you see a beautiful sunset or sunrise

DISCOVERY
is
POWERFUL

* When you find out one of your kids did something well in school
* When you exercise
* When you solve the crossword puzzle, all of it or most of it
* When you find a new recipe you like
* When you locate a great TV show while you're dial flipping
* When you enjoy a new food
* When you make a sale
* When you change your diet for the better
* When you laugh at a joke
* When you find out your favorite comedian is on TV tonight
* When you learn the best player in baseball has been traded to *your* team
* When you find out there's more in your checkbook than you thought

Every POSITIVE DISCOVERY
creates
new ENERGY

* When you get a compliment from someone
* When you get a new job
* When you learn something new
* When you find just the right gift for some-one special
* When you meet an old friend
* When you rearrange your living room
* When you figure out the murderer in a mystery
* When you find out someone loves you
* When you close on a house
* When you get the Final Jeopardy! answer
* When you start playing a new sport
* When you see that your last roll of pictures turned out great
* When you get a surprise gift
* When you recall a name you've been trying to remember

POSITIVE DISCOVERY
happens in
many ways

* When you find out you're going to be a mother -- or a father
* When you write a letter, a poem, a story
* When you paint the spare room
* When you buy a new car
* When you see a great exhibit in a museum

ENERGY
is
EXCITING

Every *POSITIVE DISCOVERY* like this -- however small -- creates *ENERGY -- ENERGY* which can help you feel *BETTER! GOOD!! TERRIFIC!!!*

How powerful is *POSITIVE DISCOVERY?*

Remember Archimedes, the ancient Greek mathematician and inventor? One day while enjoying a leisurely bath, Archimedes finally solved the scientific riddle of displacement. In an instant he understood why a heavy ship can, unlike a metal coin, float in water. He realized that so long as any vessel -- or object -- weighs less than the weight of the water it displaces, it will not sink.

So overwhelming was Archimedes' experience of *POSITIVE DISCOVERY* -- so intense the *ENERGY* which surged into his body at that moment in the 3rd century B.C. -- that he immediately leaped from his bathtub, ran right out of his house into the street, and proceeded -- despite his stark nakedness -- to excite his fellow townspeople by running up and down, exclaiming, "Eureka! Eureka!! Eureka!!!"

There is no limit to the ENERGY of POSITIVE DISCOVERY

Although most of us might feel uncomfortable imitating Archimedes, we can all experience *ENERGY* like he felt -- *ENERGY* which comes from *DISCOVERY* -- *ENERGY* which can make you feel *BETTER* -- *GOOD* -- *TERRIFIC* on a daily basis.

Want a more modern example of the power of *POSITIVE DISCOVERY?*

OK.

Meet Michael Allen, an architectural designer who, in the mid-1980's, was asked to help discover how to design a retractable roof for a 50,000-seat sports facility in Toronto, Ontario. The planners wanted a domed stadium which could be opened during fair weather -- something which had never been accomplished on a large scale before.

It was an extremely challenging problem: How could a stadium roof weighing thousands of tons be smoothly, quickly, and efficiently drawn back to let the sunshine in?

The ENERGY from POSITIVE DISCOVERY makes others' lives BETTER

As with Archimedes, the answer came to Michael Allen in an unexpected way. During a routine airline flight, Allen began playing around with the retractable airline food tray attached to the seat in front of him -- and, suddenly, his moment of *POSITIVE DISCOVERY* had arrived.

Whether Michael Allen left his seat and ran up and down the aircraft aisle in celebration has not been recorded, yet the *ENERGY* which accompanied his experience of *DISCOVERY* is there for all to see: the sports world's Toronto SkyDome where, with the flip of a switch, the mammoth roof retracts silently along rail-like tracks in only 20 minutes. No more rainouts, no more fans sitting inside on beautiful summer days. The best of both worlds.

Completed in 1989, the SkyDome attracts thousands of visitors from all over the world who admire its architecture -- and millions of sports fans who enjoy its unparalleled comfort. In fact, baseball's Blue Jays drew a record four million fans in both 1991 and 1992 with the help of SkyDome.

POSITIVE DISCOVERY
can happen
to anyone

Think of all the people -- including the Toronto Blue Jays themselves, who captured their first World Series in 1992 -- who have felt **BETTER -- GOOD -- TERRIFIC** because of Michael Allen's **POSITIVE DISCOVERY.**

Granted, we're not all mathematicians, inventors, architects, or designers. We're nurses, teachers, engineers, bankers, salespeople, parents. But the *principle* is exactly the same. We can all experience the magic of **DISCOVERY** -- and the incredible **ENERGY** it brings!!

It CAN happen to you

The key -- as both Archimedes and Michael Allen show -- is that you have to be *looking* for **DISCOVERY** in order for it to happen. Archimedes might never have solved the problem of displacement if he hadn't been thinking about it that day in his bath. Michael Allen may never have figured out how to create a retractable stadium roof if he hadn't been looking for an answer during his plane flight. To maximize the number of **POSITIVE DISCOVERIES** in your life, you must be looking for them all the time.

To a certain extent, life gives every one of us moments of DISCOVERY without us ever having to look for them. We grow up, we graduate, get married, get jobs and promotions. We move to different places, we have children and grandchildren.

But that's not enough. The **ENERGY** we experience at these huge moments of **DISCOVERY** will only sustain us so long. To achieve high energy living -- to live life at a consistently high level of energy -- we need more **DISCOVERY**.

You have to look
for
POSITIVE DISCOVERY

To create a positive growth pattern that's exhilarating -- to produce enough **ENERGY** on a daily basis to enable you to achieve what you want to accomplish *every single day* -- you need more moments of **DISCOVERY**. *Many, many more.*

How can you do this? How can you create **ENERGY** to make you feel **BETTER -- GOOD -- TERRIFIC** every day of your life? By putting your mind into a **DISCOVERY MODE.**

DISCOVER

DISCOVERY MODE

When is your mind in *DISCOVERY MODE?*

* When you look forward to something
* When you travel to a new place
* When you try a new way of doing something
* When you wear new clothes
* When you change your hairstyle
* When you introduce yourself to someone new
* When you try a new sport
* When you read a new book
* When you go to a new restaurant
* When you take risks -- mental or physical
* When you learn something new
* When you play a musical instrument
* When you listen to a new piece of music
* When you go to the movies
* When you rent a new video

A mind in DISCOVERY MODE
will encounter
POSITIVE DISCOVERIES

* When you tell someone how you feel about them
* When you try a new recipe
* When you do a crossword puzzle
* When you watch a new TV program
* When you admit you made a mistake
* When you bring home a new pet
* When you go to a museum
* When you plant a garden
* When you make a suggestion to your boss
* When you compliment someone
* When you play a new game
* When you call up an old friend
* When you say, "I have an idea!"
* When you take a picture
* When you make plans
* When you give someone a gift
* When you ask someone out on a date

You can make
POSITIVE DISCOVERIES
happen

* When you tell a joke

* When you ask someone to marry you

* When you hang a new picture in your home

* When you surprise someone

* When you get into the batter's box

* When you invite someone over for dinner

* When you enter a fishing tournament

* When you help someone

None of these activities involves history-changing inventions or developments, yet they all create opportunitites for *POSITIVE DISCOVERY* -- for surges and bursts of *ENERGY* -- for feeling *BETTER -- GOOD -- TERRIFIC!!*

Activities create opportunities for POSITIVE DISCOVERY

But you have to work for your *POSITIVE DISCOVERIES* -- to constantly create opportunities for *DISCOVERY* to happen. You can't just sit back and wait for *POSITIVE DISCOVERIES* to come your way. Sure, some will, but your overall *ENERGY* will still be low. You won't be able to live life at a high-energy level. It's like anything else: the harder you work for *DISCOVERY*, the greater will be your rewards, the more *ENERGY* you'll have.

Back to history for a moment. Thomas Edison experienced one of history's greatest moments of *POSITIVE DISCOVERY*. He didn't invent the light bulb, but in the late 1800's he did *DISCOVER* the carbon filament which raised the level of light emitted by electric bulbs to the *ENERGY* level we all can appreciate every time we turn on a light switch.

The key to Edison's illuminating *DISCOVERY* was finding just the right type of element for the filament to fully illuminate the gases inside the bulb. How hard did Edison work for this amazing *POSITIVE DISCOVERY?* He tried over *50* different filaments before discovering the right one!

Hard work = greater rewards

DISCOVERY EQUATION

The equation is simple: The harder you work to create opportunities for *DISCOVERY* in your life, the more *POSITIVE DISCOVERIES* you'll find, and the more *ENERGY* you'll have. You'll feel *BETTER -- GOOD -- TERRIFIC* more of the time, and feel more *ENERGY* on a daily basis than you ever thought possible!!!

DISCOVERY = ENERGY
ENERGY = FEELING
BETTER / GOOD / TERRIFIC!!!

Think you might be *too old* to start DISCOVERING?

Think again!

Meet George.

George is 77 years young.

Two years ago George had a wonderful *POSITIVE DISCOVERY.*

Realizing that he missed the flying he had done during World War II, George began to dream of becoming a pilot once more. His mind entered *DISCOVERY MODE.*

Looking through magazines, George became fascinated with two-man gliders. While watching gliders soar into the air at a local airport, George thought about climbing toward the clouds with one of his grandsons at his side.

George had experienced a wonderful *POSITIVE DISCOVERY*, and his mind filled with the *ENERGY* needed to begin working toward making his dream a reality.

POSITIVE DISCOVERY
can happen at any age

George went out and purchased a kit to build a two-man glider, only to learn that because of a blood pressure problem he couldn't obtain a license for that type of plane. Upon finding this out he sold the two-man glider kit.

But so powerful was the process of *POSITIVE DISCOVERY* George had initiated that, despite this setback, the surges of *ENERGY* he continued to experience drove him onward.

His mind turned in another direction. He began to think about a one-man ultralight glider which does not require a license.

It wouldn't be easy. Because George decided to build the glider from a kit.

George worked for almost TWO YEARS to give his dream substance. His *POSITIVE DISCOVERY* -- a reborn love of flying -- continued to create *ENERGY*. Despite the painstaking difficulty of constructing an entire aircraft, his mind went on *DISCOVERING* every day just how to do it!

The ENERGY from POSITIVE DISCOVERY finds its way around obstacles

And he did!!

One day George stepped back and realized that his dream had come true. He looked in amazement at a complete ultralight glider -- a glider he had built himself! And he was 75 years old!!

George's **POSITIVE DISCOVERY** was nearing fulfillment. It was time to take to the skies.

Wanting others to share in his accomplishment, George asked a friend, a local undertaker, to record the final chapter of his amazing **POSITIVE DISCOVERY** on videotape.

With the video camera rolling, George left the earth in his ultralight glider, climbing gracefully to tree level.

He was back in the sky again -- where he knew he belonged.

Watching the earth recede below him, George felt his **POSITIVE DISCOVERY** create amazing levels of **ENERGY** -- **ENERGY** that made him feel more than **TERRIFIC!** He was **EXHILARATED!!**

EXHILARATING!

And then,

abruptly,

horrifyingly,

George crashed.

His ultralight glider suddenly collided with the ground, crumpling to pieces and injuring George. After being rushed to a hospital, George had to walk on crutches for three to four weeks, and sported a swelling on his head the size of a grapefruit.

George had even more pain to endure.

Ironically, because of the videotape taken by George's friend, a large audience witnessed George's fall from the sky as it was shown on the three local TV news stations.

Their reaction? HOW TERRIBLE! HOW AWFUL! What did that crazy man think he was doing?

POSITIVE DISCOVERY
can lift us to
amazing accomplishments

George's reaction?

"Any landing you can walk away from is a good landing."

His plan for the future?

To rebuild his ultralight glider, to again rise to the heights promised by his *POSITIVE DISCOVERY!*

For me, this is a very special story.

It teaches us all many things:

How powerful *POSITIVE DISCOVERY* can be -- at any age, for anybody.

How the *ENERGY* created through *POSITIVE DISCOVERY* can propel us to remarkable achievements -- accomplishments which make us feel *BETTER -- GOOD -- TERRIFIC!*

How hard we must sometimes work to attain the goals *POSITIVE DISCOVERY* suggests to us.

POSITIVE DISCOVERY creates enough ENERGY to achieve very high goals

How *POSITIVE DISCOVERY* brings with it the *COURAGE* needed to overcome setbacks and surmount obstacles, and go on, no matter what pain we may experience along the way.

How *POSITIVE DISCOVERY* creates amazing levels of *ENERGY* to enable us to realize our dreams.

And this story is *special* for another reason.

You see, I know George personally.

He's my father-in-law.

I personally watched George transformed by his *POSITIVE DISCOVERY.*

I watched him *ENERGIZED* every day for almost two years as his dream took shape.

I watched a man, who could easily have been living in the past, filled with new *ENERGY* -- *ENERGY* which not only helped him feel *BETTER* -- *GOOD* -- *TERRIFIC*, but made all of us who are close to him feel *BETTER* -- *GOOD* -- *TERRIFIC* as well!!

ENERGIZED!!!

And, in spite of the pain of George's crash, I still see him *ENERGIZED* by his *POSITIVE DISCOVERY*, planning every day to once again reach for the sky.

For me, George is living proof of what *POSITIVE DISCOVERY* can do.

For a man supposedly well past his prime.

For me. For you .

For all of us!

Let's face it: The danger in being an adult is that the world looks too much the same to us. Each day we go to the same old places, see the same old people with the same old attitudes. We stop making *POSITIVE DISCOVERIES*, we grow bored, stale, and old ourselves. We lose *ENERGY*, we suffer distress and even disease. Our minds -- and ourselves -- become like water which never moves. After a while, we *are* stagnant pools of water -- unpleasant to look at or be near.

But it doesn't have to be this way!!

A mind in DISCOVERY MODE is always full of ENERGY

Do you enjoy sitting on a beach, watching the waves roll in?

Sure!! We all do.   It's a refreshing experience -- a feeling of constantly renewing *ENERGY.*

Those waves hitting the shore are a symbol for the constant **POSITIVE DISCOVERIES** which come to a mind which is in **DISCOVERY MODE.** If you constantly seek out new experiences, make positive changes in your life, look at life in new ways, you will experience ongoing waves of **DISCOVERY** -- a never-ceasing stream of **ENERGY** to help you feel **BETTER -- GOOD -- TERRIFIC!!!**

BETTER -- GOOD -- TERRIFIC

How often should your mind be in *DISCOVERY MODE?*

Some of the time?

More than that.

Most of the time?

Still not good enough.

All of the time?

ABSOLUTELY!!!

Is the world really interesting enough to provide us with constant *POSITIVE DISCOVERIES* to keep our minds functioning at a high level of *ENERGY?* Definitely. It's just that, unlike our children, we've stopped seeing it that way. As the philosopher Nietzsche expressed it, "Is not life a hundred times too short for us to bore ourselves?"

Let's look at an example of *POSITIVE DISCOVERY* in the workplace -- of the importance of being in *DISCOVERY MODE* at your job as well.

DISCOVER all of the time

Meet Ellen, whose company, like many others these days, is changing rapidly.

During the past few months Ellen has seen many changes at work. One whole department has been phased out, and several of Ellen's friends have been transferred to other divisions within the company -- including Sam, whom Ellen worked with for almost eight years.

New people have been added in key positions. Ellen herself has been asked to take on new responsibilities -- including publishing the company's newsletter.

She's been moved to a different office, one without the window she had in her old work area. She now has to share a secretary with two other people, and the company wants her to start using a new desktop computer system.

Ellen also has to attend weekly training sessions to learn new skills. The company even wants her to take a couple of classes at a local college on time management and personal efficiency.

CHANGES can be viewed as POSITIVE or NEGATIVE DISCOVERIES

Some of Ellen's co-workers did not react positively to these changes. In fact, you'll meet one of them in the second part of this book.

Ellen felt differently. Understanding the importance of being constantly in **DISCOVERY MODE** -- even at work -- she saw the changes in her work life as opportunities for growth, for **POSITIVE DISCOVERY** -- for new **ENERGY.** She made the *CHOICE* to see the changes in her company as **POSITIVE DISCOVERIES.**

Shortly after the personnel changes in her office, Ellen made a special effort to introduce herself to all of the new people over the course of a week or two. She discovered that one of the new workers, Jim, shared an interest in tennis, and had even played professionally for a short time.

Ellen started playing tennis with Jim once a week and received many helpful hints on how to improve her game -- especially her backhand. Ellen's tennis improved dramatically -- she even won a game against Jim from time to time. Playing tennis more also improved Ellen's health and gave her more **ENERGY** every day!

POSITIVE DISCOVERIES
are at work -- for those who look

Faced with a heavier work load every day, Ellen voluntarily cut her lunch hour from one hour to thirty minutes, eating less in the process. She discovered Shirley, another new face, at one of the company's retraining sessions. Shirley taught Ellen about healthy food alternatives which would help her feel *BETTER*. Eating less for lunch every day, Ellen found she had more *ENERGY* than ever to get through her busier afternoons.

Although Ellen missed the window in her old office, she decorated her new workspace with posters of countries she'd always wanted to visit. One of these posters, a scene of skiing in the French Alps, attracted the attention of Wendy, one of the new word processors in the office, who told Ellen how she could spend a week in Europe for less money than she ever believed possible. She had another *POSITIVE DISCOVERY* while at work -- and even more *ENERGY!*

Ellen began to review the manuals and information on the new desktop computer system, and discovered the company would make a unit available to her for home use free of charge. Ellen would then be able to work some of her 40 hour workload at home. Ellen took the company up

POSITIVE DISCOVERY is cumulative: each one fuels the next

on its offer, and steadily mastered the new technology. She realized she would now be able to use the desktop system to publish a downhill skiing newsletter at home, and network with other people across the country who shared her interest in skiing -- including Sam, the friend who'd been transferred to another state. Another *POSITIVE DISCOVERY* -- another surge of *ENERGY!*

Using what she learned in her courses on time management and personal efficiency, Ellen began incorporating a regular column on these topics in the company's monthly newsletter. Many of her co-workers thanked her for the advice she offered, and she even attracted the attention of her supervisor, who praised her in a company memo.

As time went on, Ellen became an even more *POSITIVE* influence on her fellow employees. She found herself being considered for promotional opportunities. Ellen has more *ENERGY* every day at work than she ever imagined possible, and never seems to have a bad day at the office.

POSITIVE DISCOVERIES
are all around you

Ellen's success is simply explained. She made the *CHOICE* to accept the many changes she experienced at work as potentially **POSITIVE DISCOVERIES** -- as opportunities to change, to grow, to feel **BETTER** and to have more **ENERGY.**

Because Ellen was willing to keep herself constantly in **DISCOVERY MODE** at her job, she benefited from a series of **POSITIVE DISCOVERIES** which made her feel **BETTER -- GOOD -- TERRIFIC!!!**

It would have been all too easy for Ellen to have closed her mind to the changes occurring in her work world, but she *CHOSE* to see those changes as potential sources of new **ENERGY.** With her mind constantly in **DISCOVERY MODE**, she worked hard to create possibilities for **POSITIVE DISCOVERY** amid the changes happening around her, and reaped BIG BENEFITS as a result.

POSITIVE DISCOVERY
reaps
BIG BENEFITS

To see if your own mind is in constant *DISCOVERY MODE,* try this simple test anytime. The next time you see a flock of birds overhead, look up.

Take a good look.

Do you feel a small surge of **ENERGY**, a moment of **DISCOVERY?**

If your mind is truly in **DISCOVERY MODE**, you will. The sight of living creatures in flight is always surprising and beautiful, and that moment of **POSITIVE DISCOVERY** should give you new **ENERGY**. You should feel **BETTER**.

You can easily put your mind into DISCOVERY MODE

If you don't feel better, start moving your mind into *DISCOVERY MODE.* Try new experiences, make constructive changes in your life, open your mind and yourself to the world around you.

The *ENERGY* of each new *POSITIVE DISCOVERY* will fuel the next.

And the next.

And the next.

Before long you'll be living and loving and accomplishing things with more *ENERGY* than ever before.

You'll feel . . . .

BETTER!

GOOD!!

TERRIFIC!!!

You can get
ENERGY
from POSITIVE DISCOVERY
every single day

SUMMARY

Every human being wants to feel *BETTER.*

You do. I do. We all do.

One of the ways this can happen on a daily basis is through *POSITIVE DISCOVERY.*

Each time you *DISCOVER* something POSITIVE in your life, your body creates *ENERGY -- ENERGY* that can help you feel *BETTER -- GOOD -- TERRIFIC!!!*

To experience many *POSITIVE DISCOVERIES* in life, your mind should be in a constant *DISCOVERY MODE.*

Being in *DISCOVERY MODE* means the willingness to take risks, to make changes, to challenge yourself, to reach out, to look at yourself and life in new and exciting ways.

The reward of always being in *DISCOVERY MODE* is having abundant *ENERGY -- ENERGY* to accomplish what you want in life, *ENERGY* to help you live life at higher and higher levels of enjoyment and accomplishment.

You'll feel

BETTER!

GOOD!!

TERRIFIC!!!

If you **DISCOVER.**

But . . .

This book is more about **ACTION** than words, right?

Right!

So let's put the theories in Part I to work in your life right away.

For the next thirty days, make **POSITIVE DISCOVERY** more a part of your life. Take some chances, make some changes, learn new things, expand your mind every chance you get.

Use the charts on the next several pages to monitor your progress in increasing **POSITIVE DISCOVERIES** in your day-to-day life.

List each **POSITIVE DISCOVERY** -- no matter how small -- in the first column. (Use other sheets of paper if you have more than five **POSITIVE DISCOVERIES** in a day.)

In the second column, describe how you helped make that **POSITIVE DISCOVERY** happen -- how you were in **DISCOVERY MODE**.

Finally, use the number continuum to the right to show how each **POSITIVE DISCOVERY** made you feel: **BETTER -- GOOD -- TERRIFIC!!!** Circle one number for each **POSITIVE DISCOVERY.** A "3" or a "4" would indicate somewhere between **BETTER -- GOOD**, while a "9" would clearly be **TERRIFIC!**

Got the idea?

GOOD!

If you're truly putting yourself more and more into **DISCOVERY MODE**, you might see something like this by DAY #20 on the next page.

You can easily increase
POSITIVE DISCOVERIES
in your life

POSITIVE DISCOVERY LOG (exhibit A)

Day #20

Date: _____

POSITIVE DISCOVERY	ACTION (How did you help it happen?)	HOW DID IT MAKE YOU FEEL?
1. Saw beautiful sunset while driving home	-------------	1 2 ③④ 5 6 7 8 9 10 (circle one)
2. Received letter from friend in Idaho		1 2 3 4 5 ⑥ 7 8 9 10 (circle one)
3. Watched son hit home run in Little League game	Helped son work on swing; pitched batting practice	1 2 3 4 5 6 7 8 ⑨ 10 (circle one)
4. Finally had a par on wicked dogleg #7 at golf course	Took lessons for first time to help correct slice	1 2 3 4 5 6 ⑦ 8 9 10 (circle one)
5. Praised by boss for ideas to improve office efficiency	Read magazine article on highly efficient offices	1 2 3 4 5 6 7 ⑧ 9 10 (circle one)

POSITIVE DISCOVERY LOG (exhibit B)

Date: _____

Day # 1

POSITIVE DISCOVERY	ACTION	HOW DID IT MAKE YOU FEEL?
	(How did you help it happen?)	BETTER-GOOD-TERRIFIC

1. _____ _____ 1 2 3 4 5 6 7 8 9 10
   _____ _____ (circle one)

2. _____ _____ 1 2 3 4 5 6 7 8 9 10
   _____ _____ (circle one)

3. _____ _____ 1 2 3 4 5 6 7 8 9 10
   _____ _____ (circle one)

4. _____ _____ 1 2 3 4 5 6 7 8 9 10
   _____ _____ (circle one)

5. _____ _____ 1 2 3 4 5 6 7 8 9 10
   _____ _____ (circle one)

POSITIVE DISCOVERY LOG (exhibit B)

Day # 2

Date: _____

POSITIVE DISCOVERY	ACTION (How did you help it happen?)	HOW DID IT MAKE YOU FEEL? BETTER-GOOD-TERRIFIC
1. _____	_____	1 2 3 4 5 6 7 8 9 10 (circle one)
2. _____	_____	1 2 3 4 5 6 7 8 9 10 (circle one)
3. _____	_____	1 2 3 4 5 6 7 8 9 10 (circle one)
4. _____	_____	1 2 3 4 5 6 7 8 9 10 (circle one)
5. _____	_____	1 2 3 4 5 6 7 8 9 10 (circle one)

POSITIVE DISCOVERY LOG (exhibit B)

Day # 3   Date: _____

POSITIVE DISCOVERY	ACTION (How did you help it happen?)	HOW DID IT MAKE YOU FEEL? BETTER-GOOD-TERRIFIC
1. _____	_____	1 2 3 4 5 6 7 8 9 10 (circle one)
2. _____	_____	1 2 3 4 5 6 7 8 9 10 (circle one)
3. _____	_____	1 2 3 4 5 6 7 8 9 10 (circle one)
4. _____	_____	1 2 3 4 5 6 7 8 9 10 (circle one)
5. _____	_____	1 2 3 4 5 6 7 8 9 10 (circle one)

POSITIVE DISCOVERY LOG (exhibit B)

Day # 4

Date: _____

POSITIVE DISCOVERY	ACTION (How did you help it happen?)	HOW DID IT MAKE YOU FEEL? *BETTER-GOOD-TERRIFIC*
1. _____	_____	1 2 3 4 5 6 7 8 9 10 (circle one)
2. _____	_____	1 2 3 4 5 6 7 8 9 10 (circle one)
3. _____	_____	1 2 3 4 5 6 7 8 9 10 (circle one)
4. _____	_____	1 2 3 4 5 6 7 8 9 10 (circle one)
5. _____	_____	1 2 3 4 5 6 7 8 9 10 (circle one)

POSITIVE DISCOVERY LOG (exhibit B)

Date: _____

Day # 5

POSITIVE DISCOVERY

ACTION
(How did you help it happen?)

**HOW DID IT MAKE
YOU FEEL?**
BETTER-GOOD-TERRIFIC

1. _____ _____ 1 2 3 4 5 6 7 8 9 10

(circle one)

2. _____ _____ 1 2 3 4 5 6 7 8 9 10

(circle one)

3. _____ _____ 1 2 3 4 5 6 7 8 9 10

(circle one)

4. _____ _____ 1 2 3 4 5 6 7 8 9 10

(circle one)

5. _____ _____ 1 2 3 4 5 6 7 8 9 10

(circle one)

POSITIVE DISCOVERY LOG (exhibit B)

Day # 6

Date: _____

	POSITIVE DISCOVERY	ACTION (How did you help it happen?)	HOW DID IT MAKE YOU FEEL? *BETTER-GOOD-TERRIFIC*
1.	_____	_____	1 2 3 4 5 6 7 8 9 10 (circle one)
2.	_____	_____	1 2 3 4 5 6 7 8 9 10 (circle one)
3.	_____	_____	1 2 3 4 5 6 7 8 9 10 (circle one)
4.	_____	_____	1 2 3 4 5 6 7 8 9 10 (circle one)
5.	_____	_____	1 2 3 4 5 6 7 8 9 10 (circle one)

POSITIVE DISCOVERY LOG (exhibit B)

Date: _____

Day # 7

POSITIVE DISCOVERY	ACTION (How did you help it happen?)	HOW DID IT MAKE YOU FEEL? *BETTER-GOOD-TERRIFIC*
1. _____	_____	1 2 3 4 5 6 7 8 9 10 (circle one)
2. _____	_____	1 2 3 4 5 6 7 8 9 10 (circle one)
3. _____	_____	1 2 3 4 5 6 7 8 9 10 (circle one)
4. _____	_____	1 2 3 4 5 6 7 8 9 10 (circle one)
5. _____	_____	1 2 3 4 5 6 7 8 9 10 (circle one)

POSITIVE DISCOVERY LOG (exhibit B)

Day # 8

Date: _____

POSITIVE DISCOVERY	ACTION (How did you help it happen?)	HOW DID IT MAKE YOU FEEL? *BETTER-GOOD-TERRIFIC*
1.		1 2 3 4 5 6 7 8 9 10 (circle one)
2.		1 2 3 4 5 6 7 8 9 10 (circle one)
3.		1 2 3 4 5 6 7 8 9 10 (circle one)
4.		1 2 3 4 5 6 7 8 9 10 (circle one)
5.		1 2 3 4 5 6 7 8 9 10 (circle one)

POSITIVE DISCOVERY LOG (exhibit B)

Day # 9

Date: _____

POSITIVE DISCOVERY	ACTION (How did you help it happen?)	HOW DID IT MAKE YOU FEEL? *BETTER-GOOD-TERRIFIC*
1. _____	_____	1 2 3 4 5 6 7 8 9 10 (circle one)
2. _____	_____	1 2 3 4 5 6 7 8 9 10 (circle one)
3. _____	_____	1 2 3 4 5 6 7 8 9 10 (circle one)
4. _____	_____	1 2 3 4 5 6 7 8 9 10 (circle one)
5. _____	_____	1 2 3 4 5 6 7 8 9 10 (circle one)

POSITIVE DISCOVERY LOG (exhibit B)

Day # 1 0

Date: _____

POSITIVE DISCOVERY	ACTION (How did you help it happen?)	HOW DID IT MAKE YOU FEEL? *BETTER-GOOD-TERRIFIC*
1. _____	_____	1 2 3 4 5 6 7 8 9 10 (circle one)
2. _____	_____	1 2 3 4 5 6 7 8 9 10 (circle one)
3. _____	_____	1 2 3 4 5 6 7 8 9 10 (circle one)
4. _____	_____	1 2 3 4 5 6 7 8 9 10 (circle one)
5. _____	_____	1 2 3 4 5 6 7 8 9 10 (circle one)

POSITIVE DISCOVERY LOG (exhibit B)

Day # 1 1   Date: _____

POSITIVE DISCOVERY	ACTION (How did you help it happen?)	HOW DID IT MAKE YOU FEEL? BETTER-GOOD-TERRIFIC
1. _____	_____	1 2 3 4 5 6 7 8 9 10 (circle one)
2. _____	_____	1 2 3 4 5 6 7 8 9 10 (circle one)
3. _____	_____	1 2 3 4 5 6 7 8 9 10 (circle one)
4. _____	_____	1 2 3 4 5 6 7 8 9 10 (circle one)
5. _____	_____	1 2 3 4 5 6 7 8 9 10 (circle one)

POSITIVE DISCOVERY LOG (exhibit B)

Day # 12

Date: _____

POSITIVE DISCOVERY	ACTION (How did you help it happen?)	HOW DID IT MAKE YOU FEEL? *BETTER-GOOD-TERRIFIC*
1. _____	_____	1 2 3 4 5 6 7 8 9 10 (circle one)
2. _____	_____	1 2 3 4 5 6 7 8 9 10 (circle one)
3. _____	_____	1 2 3 4 5 6 7 8 9 10 (circle one)
4. _____	_____	1 2 3 4 5 6 7 8 9 10 (circle one)
5. _____	_____	1 2 3 4 5 6 7 8 9 10 (circle one)

POSITIVE DISCOVERY LOG (exhibit B)

Day # 1 3

Date: _____

POSITIVE DISCOVERY	ACTION	HOW DID IT MAKE YOU FEEL?
	(How did you help it happen?)	*BETTER-GOOD-TERRIFIC*

1. _____ _____   1 2 3 4 5 6 7 8 9 10
   (circle one)

2. _____ _____   1 2 3 4 5 6 7 8 9 10
   (circle one)

3. _____ _____   1 2 3 4 5 6 7 8 9 10
   (circle one)

4. _____ _____   1 2 3 4 5 6 7 8 9 10
   (circle one)

5. _____ _____   1 2 3 4 5 6 7 8 9 10
   (circle one)

POSITIVE DISCOVERY LOG (exhibit B)

Day #14

Date: _____

POSITIVE DISCOVERY	ACTION (How did you help it happen?)	HOW DID IT MAKE YOU FEEL? *BETTER-GOOD-TERRIFIC*
1. _____	_____	1 2 3 4 5 6 7 8 9 10 (circle one)
2. _____	_____	1 2 3 4 5 6 7 8 9 10 (circle one)
3. _____	_____	1 2 3 4 5 6 7 8 9 10 (circle one)
4. _____	_____	1 2 3 4 5 6 7 8 9 10 (circle one)
5. _____	_____	1 2 3 4 5 6 7 8 9 10 (circle one)

POSITIVE DISCOVERY LOG (exhibit B)

Date: _____

Day # 1 5

POSITIVE DISCOVERY	ACTION (How did you help it happen?)	HOW DID IT MAKE YOU FEEL? *BETTER-GOOD-TERRIFIC*
1. _____	_____	1 2 3 4 5 6 7 8 9 10 (circle one)
2. _____	_____	1 2 3 4 5 6 7 8 9 10 (circle one)
3. _____	_____	1 2 3 4 5 6 7 8 9 10 (circle one)
4. _____	_____	1 2 3 4 5 6 7 8 9 10 (circle one)
5. _____	_____	1 2 3 4 5 6 7 8 9 10 (circle one)

POSITIVE DISCOVERY LOG (exhibit B)

Day # 16

Date: _____

POSITIVE DISCOVERY	ACTION (How did you help it happen?)	HOW DID IT MAKE YOU FEEL? *BETTER-GOOD-TERRIFIC*
1. _____	_____	1 2 3 4 5 6 7 8 9 10 (circle one)
2. _____	_____	1 2 3 4 5 6 7 8 9 10 (circle one)
3. _____	_____	1 2 3 4 5 6 7 8 9 10 (circle one)
4. _____	_____	1 2 3 4 5 6 7 8 9 10 (circle one)
5. _____	_____	1 2 3 4 5 6 7 8 9 10 (circle one)

POSITIVE DISCOVERY LOG (exhibit B)

Day # 17

Date: _____

POSITIVE DISCOVERY	ACTION (How did you help it happen?)	HOW DID IT MAKE YOU FEEL? BETTER-GOOD-TERRIFIC
1. _____	_____	1 2 3 4 5 6 7 8 9 10 (circle one)
2. _____	_____	1 2 3 4 5 6 7 8 9 10 (circle one)
3. _____	_____	1 2 3 4 5 6 7 8 9 10 (circle one)
4. _____	_____	1 2 3 4 5 6 7 8 9 10 (circle one)
5. _____	_____	1 2 3 4 5 6 7 8 9 10 (circle one)

POSITIVE DISCOVERY LOG (exhibit B)

Day # 18

Date: _____

POSITIVE DISCOVERY	ACTION (How did you help it happen?)	HOW DID IT MAKE YOU FEEL? *BETTER-GOOD-TERRIFIC*
1. _____	_____	1 2 3 4 5 6 7 8 9 10 (circle one)
2. _____	_____	1 2 3 4 5 6 7 8 9 10 (circle one)
3. _____	_____	1 2 3 4 5 6 7 8 9 10 (circle one)
4. _____	_____	1 2 3 4 5 6 7 8 9 10 (circle one)
5. _____	_____	1 2 3 4 5 6 7 8 9 10 (circle one)

POSITIVE DISCOVERY LOG (exhibit B)

Day # 1 9

Date: _____

POSITIVE DISCOVERY	ACTION (How did you help it happen?)	HOW DID IT MAKE YOU FEEL? *BETTER-GOOD-TERRIFIC*
1. _____	_____	1 2 3 4 5 6 7 8 9 10 (circle one)
2. _____	_____	1 2 3 4 5 6 7 8 9 10 (circle one)
3. _____	_____	1 2 3 4 5 6 7 8 9 10 (circle one)
4. _____	_____	1 2 3 4 5 6 7 8 9 10 (circle one)
5. _____	_____	1 2 3 4 5 6 7 8 9 10 (circle one)

POSITIVE DISCOVERY LOG (exhibit B)

Day # 20

Date: _____

POSITIVE DISCOVERY	ACTION (How did you help it happen?)	HOW DID IT MAKE YOU FEEL? BETTER-GOOD-TERRIFIC
1. _____	_____	1 2 3 4 5 6 7 8 9 10 (circle one)
2. _____	_____	1 2 3 4 5 6 7 8 9 10 (circle one)
3. _____	_____	1 2 3 4 5 6 7 8 9 10 (circle one)
4. _____	_____	1 2 3 4 5 6 7 8 9 10 (circle one)
5. _____	_____	1 2 3 4 5 6 7 8 9 10 (circle one)

POSITIVE DISCOVERY LOG (exhibit B)

Day # 2 1   Date: _____

POSITIVE DISCOVERY	ACTION (How did you help it happen?)	HOW DID IT MAKE YOU FEEL? *BETTER-GOOD-TERRIFIC*
1. _____	_____	1 2 3 4 5 6 7 8 9 10 (circle one)
2. _____	_____	1 2 3 4 5 6 7 8 9 10 (circle one)
3. _____	_____	1 2 3 4 5 6 7 8 9 10 (circle one)
4. _____	_____	1 2 3 4 5 6 7 8 9 10 (circle one)
5. _____	_____	1 2 3 4 5 6 7 8 9 10 (circle one)

POSITIVE DISCOVERY LOG (exhibit B)

Day # 22

Date: _____

POSITIVE DISCOVERY	ACTION (How did you help it happen?)	HOW DID IT MAKE YOU FEEL? BETTER-GOOD-TERRIFIC
1. _____	_____	1 2 3 4 5 6 7 8 9 10 (circle one)
2. _____	_____	1 2 3 4 5 6 7 8 9 10 (circle one)
3. _____	_____	1 2 3 4 5 6 7 8 9 10 (circle one)
4. _____	_____	1 2 3 4 5 6 7 8 9 10 (circle one)
5. _____	_____	1 2 3 4 5 6 7 8 9 10 (circle one)

POSITIVE DISCOVERY LOG (exhibit B)

Day # 23

Date: _____

POSITIVE DISCOVERY	ACTION (How did you help it happen?)	HOW DID IT MAKE YOU FEEL? BETTER-GOOD-TERRIFIC
1. _____	_____	1 2 3 4 5 6 7 8 9 10 (circle one)
2. _____	_____	1 2 3 4 5 6 7 8 9 10 (circle one)
3. _____	_____	1 2 3 4 5 6 7 8 9 10 (circle one)
4. _____	_____	1 2 3 4 5 6 7 8 9 10 (circle one)
5. _____	_____	1 2 3 4 5 6 7 8 9 10 (circle one)

POSITIVE DISCOVERY LOG (exhibit B)

Day # 2 4

Date: _____

POSITIVE DISCOVERY	ACTION (How did you help it happen?)	HOW DID IT MAKE YOU FEEL? BETTER-GOOD-TERRIFIC
1.	_____	1 2 3 4 5 6 7 8 9 10 (circle one)
2.	_____	1 2 3 4 5 6 7 8 9 10 (circle one)
3.	_____	1 2 3 4 5 6 7 8 9 10 (circle one)
4.	_____	1 2 3 4 5 6 7 8 9 10 (circle one)
5.	_____	1 2 3 4 5 6 7 8 9 10 (circle one)

POSITIVE DISCOVERY LOG (exhibit B)

Day # 2 5   Date: _____

POSITIVE DISCOVERY	ACTION (How did you help it happen?)	HOW DID IT MAKE YOU FEEL? *BETTER-GOOD-TERRIFIC*
1. _____	_____	1 2 3 4 5 6 7 8 9 10
		(circle one)
2. _____	_____	1 2 3 4 5 6 7 8 9 10
		(circle one)
3. _____	_____	1 2 3 4 5 6 7 8 9 10
		(circle one)
4. _____	_____	1 2 3 4 5 6 7 8 9 10
		(circle one)
5. _____	_____	1 2 3 4 5 6 7 8 9 10
		(circle one)

POSITIVE DISCOVERY LOG (exhibit B)

Day # 26

Date: _____

POSITIVE DISCOVERY	ACTION (How did you help it happen?)	HOW DID IT MAKE YOU FEEL? *BETTER-GOOD-TERRIFIC*
1. _____	_____ _____	1 2 3 4 5 6 7 8 9 10 (circle one)
2. _____	_____ _____	1 2 3 4 5 6 7 8 9 10 (circle one)
3. _____	_____ _____	1 2 3 4 5 6 7 8 9 10 (circle one)
4. _____	_____ _____	1 2 3 4 5 6 7 8 9 10 (circle one)
5. _____	_____ _____	1 2 3 4 5 6 7 8 9 10 (circle one)

Date: _____

Day # 2 7

POSITIVE DISCOVERY	ACTION (How did you help it happen?)	HOW DID IT MAKE YOU FEEL? *BETTER-GOOD-TERRIFIC*
1. _____	_____	1 2 3 4 5 6 7 8 9 10 (circle one)
2. _____	_____	1 2 3 4 5 6 7 8 9 10 (circle one)
3. _____	_____	1 2 3 4 5 6 7 8 9 10 (circle one)
4. _____	_____	1 2 3 4 5 6 7 8 9 10 (circle one)
5. _____	_____	1 2 3 4 5 6 7 8 9 10 (circle one)

POSITIVE DISCOVERY LOG (exhibit B)

Day #28

Date: _____

POSITIVE DISCOVERY	ACTION (How did you help it happen?)	HOW DID IT MAKE YOU FEEL? BETTER-GOOD-TERRIFIC
1. _____	_____	1 2 3 4 5 6 7 8 9 10 (circle one)
2. _____	_____	1 2 3 4 5 6 7 8 9 10 (circle one)
3. _____	_____	1 2 3 4 5 6 7 8 9 10 (circle one)
4. _____	_____	1 2 3 4 5 6 7 8 9 10 (circle one)
5. _____	_____	1 2 3 4 5 6 7 8 9 10 (circle one)

POSITIVE DISCOVERY LOG (exhibit B)

Day # 29

Date: _____

POSITIVE DISCOVERY

ACTION
(How did you help it happen?)

HOW DID IT MAKE
YOU FEEL?
BETTER-GOOD-TERRIFIC

1. _____ _____ 1 2 3 4 5 6 7 8 9 10

(circle one)

2. _____ _____ 1 2 3 4 5 6 7 8 9 10

(circle one)

3. _____ _____ 1 2 3 4 5 6 7 8 9 10

(circle one)

4. _____ _____ 1 2 3 4 5 6 7 8 9 10

(circle one)

5. _____ _____ 1 2 3 4 5 6 7 8 9 10

(circle one)

POSITIVE DISCOVERY LOG (exhibit B)

Day # 3 0   Date: _____

POSITIVE DISCOVERY	ACTION (How did you help it happen?)	HOW DID IT MAKE YOU FEEL? BETTER-GOOD-TERRIFIC
1.	_____	1 2 3 4 5 6 7 8 9 10 (circle one)
2.	_____	1 2 3 4 5 6 7 8 9 10 (circle one)
3.	_____	1 2 3 4 5 6 7 8 9 10 (circle one)
4.	_____	1 2 3 4 5 6 7 8 9 10 (circle one)
5.	_____	1 2 3 4 5 6 7 8 9 10 (circle one)

PART II

NEGATIVE DISCOVERY

But . . .

What about the bad things that happen to us in life?

The **NEGATIVE DISCOVERIES.**

Obviously, not all of the **DISCOVERIES** we experience are **POSITIVE.** In fact, we all must deal with the other side of the coin -- **NEGATIVE DISCOVERY** -- just about every day of our lives.

You know what it's like.

Your mechanic calls and says that $100 repair is now going to cost five times that much.

Your boss calls you in -- and you don't get the raise, or worse, you're fired.

Your doctor tells you: "Your physical didn't come back OK."

The stock market falls 100 points.

A client calls you back to cancel that big sale.

Life gives us NEGATIVE as well as POSITIVE DISCOVERIES

A patient tells you that you don't know your job.

One of your kids breaks a leg at school.

The phone rings, and the voice at the other end tells you that someone close to you has died.

How do we *feel* at these moments?

TERRIFIC? No way.

GOOD? Not even close.

BETTER? Forget it.

NEGATIVE DISCOVERY reduces our level of ENERGY

Let's face it -- we feel *BAD*, even *TERRIBLE*. **NEGATIVE DISCOVERY** causes a "hit" which reduces our level of **ENERGY**. If the "hit" is severe enough -- devastating -- you feel that all your ENERGY is gone. You're paralyzed. You can't seem to think, feel, move, or do anything. "The Nerves sit ceremonious, like Tombs," as the poet Emily Dickinson perfectly put it.

PRINCIPLE OF - DISCOVERY

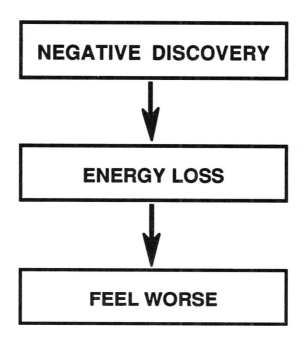

You don't feel a surge or burst of *ENERGY,* but just the opposite. If your *ENERGY* level continues to drop, you will suffer distress. And if the distress continues you may experience disease.

What do you do? When *NEGATIVE DISCOVERY* happens, what next?

The answer: **TAKE AN ACTION.**

You'll feel *BETTER.*

In 1992, Kenny Lofton, a baseball player for the Cleveland Indians, had a marvelous first season in the American League. He hit .285 (in baseball terms, almost *TERRIFIC*), stole 66 bases (definitely *TERRIFIC*), and made many highlight-film catches in the outfield (clearly *TERRIFIC*). His season was a series of *POSITIVE DISCOVERIES* -- so much so that many people, including Kenny himself, felt that he should be named the American League's Rookie of the Year.

When you have a NEGATIVE DISCOVERY TAKE AN ACTION

But, when the award was announced following the season, Kenny didn't win. Someone else did. Kenny Lofton experienced a **NEGATIVE DISCOVERY** that day he got the news. He took a huge "hit" against his **ENERGY** level.

How did he feel?

BAD? Probably.

TERRIBLE. Good chance.

But what did he do?

He took an **ACTION.**

He climbed in his car and drove to the top of a mountain near his home in Arizona. There he could be alone.

He got out of his car. He stood outside and let out the longest, loudest scream he could manage.

Did this mean he got the award? Of course not.

When NEGATIVE DISCOVERY "hits" you, ACT to restore your ENERGY

But, did he feel *BETTER?*

Definitely.

Did he feel *GOOD?*

Probably not.

Did he feel *TERRIFIC?*

No way.

But he **did feel** *BETTER* -- because he *TOOK AN ACTION.*

How many of us when life "hits" us with a *NEGATIVE DISCOVERY* just sit there, feeling worse and worse and worse?

Let's face it -- it would be *TERRIFIC* if living didn't involve *NEGATIVE DISCOVERY.* But it does. *NEGATIVE DISCOVERY* cannot be avoided. Life is going to send *NEGATIVE DISCOVERIES* your way -- you know that, and you must be prepared to deal with them.

NEGATIVE DISCOVERY
is all around us

You deal with **NEGATIVE DISCOVERY** by *TAKING ACTION.*

Let's take an all-too common scenario: you find out you've lost your job.

You feel **BAD -- TERRIBLE.**

You can sit at home and continue to <u>**feel**</u> **TERRIBLE**, inviting distress and even disease, or you can *TAKE ACTION.*

* Talk to a friend
* See a career counselor
* Ask your family for support
* Start looking for other jobs

You're still out of work. You won't feel TERRIFIC and you probably won't feel GOOD -- but you will feel *BETTER.*

If the stock market falls 100 points,
> *TAKE AN ACTION*:
>> Review your investment portfolio.

If you don't ACT
after a NEGATIVE DISCOVERY
you'll lose more ENERGY

If your physical isn't OK,
> **TAKE AN ACTION:**
>> Consult with your doctor about possible treatments.

If you receive an outlandish bill,
> **TAKE AN ACTION:**
>> Call the company and ask them to check the bill's accuracy. Even if the bill's correct and you have to pay, you'll feel **BETTER**.

If you break something at home,
> **TAKE AN ACTION:**
>> Try to repair it, or buy a replacement. If you allow yourself to dwell on the loss of **ENERGY** which happened when the item broke, you will only lose more **ENERGY**.

If you don't get the raise,
> **TAKE AN ACTION:**
>> Rearrange your finances to minimize the effect of not getting the raise, or apply for other jobs.

Take
an
ACTION

Even in the most-feared circumstances, taking action will always make you feel **BETTER.** Not GOOD or TERRIFIC, but definitely **BETTER.**

Let's take many people's worst fear of all.

Someone close to you dies.

There are no words to describe how **BAD** you **feel.** You're nowhere near GOOD -- TERRIFIC. Those states of mind seem so far away that you feel you may never experience them again.

Following a **NEGATIVE DISCOVERY** this devastating, we feel totally without energy, listless, dead. And, in a way, we are dead, since in the strict scientific sense death equals the absence of ENERGY. To come back to life, to start **ENERGY** again flowing in your system, you must **TAKE ACTION** -- even when life "hits" you this hard.

What can you do?

Even a small ACTION after a NEGATIVE DISCOVERY will = FEELING BETTER

Call a friend or relative.

Send flowers or a charitable contribution.

Attend the funeral.

Talk openly with others about what you feel.

Write down memories of the person you lost.

If you do these things, will you feel GOOD? Not likely. Will you feel TERRIFIC? Not a chance.

But you will feel *BETTER*.

Even taking a small *ACTION* after a huge *NEGATIVE DISCOVERY* will result in feeling *BETTER*. And as you start to feel *BETTER,* your *ENERGY* will slowly return.

The *PRINCIPLE OF ACTION* teaches us: No matter what kind of *NEGATIVE DISCOVERY* you experience, you will feel *BETTER* if you *TAKE* ACTION -- an *ACTION* that is constructive, positive, and appropriate.

To grow beyond the pain
of NEGATIVE DISCOVERY
take ACTION

When the composer Johannes Brahms lost his mother, he was almost destroyed. Their relationship was unusually close, and he could not imagine continuing his life without her. Yet, despite his pain, he knew that work was the antidote.

He **TOOK ACTION.**

Brahms threw himself into a huge new musical composition, the German <u>Requiem</u>, which, when completed not long after his mother's death, was hailed as his greatest work to date. Despite experiencing the death of a loved one -- perhaps life's worst "hit" against our **ENERGY** -- Brahms took ACTION and was able to rise to new heights of personal and artisitc growth.

Ask yourself this:

If you noticed a plant in your home which was very dry, what would you do?

Water it, or course!

If you noticed a light bulb burned out somewhere in your home, what would you do?

ACTION
is the KEY

Replace it, of course!

If you saw that your car's gas gauge was touching "Empty", what would you do?

Go to a gas station, or course!

In each of these situations, something has, in a very real sense, taken a negative "hit" in your life. Something in your life has experienced a small **NEGATIVE DISCOVERY.**

But in each case you **TOOK ACTION** to make the situation **BETTER.**

Then why not treat YOURSELF the same way?

How many of us are dragging through life low on water, burned out, needing fuel -- because we don't TAKE ACTION to restore our own ENERGY?

No matter what **NEGATIVE DISCOVERY** life sends your way, you can feel **BETTER** as long as you **TAKE ACTION.**

ACTION
counteracts
NEGATIVE DISCOVERY

If you're a few pounds overweight,
>*TAKE ACTION:*
>>Start exercising. Adjust your diet.

If you're always late for work,
>*TAKE ACTION*:
>>Get up earlier. Do things the night before that you normally do in the morning.

If you're charging too much on your credit card,
>*TAKE ACTION:*
>>Take only a set amount of cash with you when you go shopping. Determine a monthly limit for charges.   Or, if the problem is extremely serious, consult a credit counselor.

Now let's consider **NEGATIVE DISCOVERY** in the workplace -- a very common situation in today's rapidly changing business environment.

Remember Ellen, from the first part of this book, whose company asked her to accept a variety of changes -- from new work tasks, to a new office, to new technology and new co-workers?

CHANGES are only
NEGATIVE DISCOVERIES
if we view them that way

Remember how Ellen was able to transform the changes in her company into *POSITIVE DISCOVERIES* -- into more and more ENERGY which helped her feel *BETTER* -- *GOOD* -- *TERRIFIC* every day on the job?

Now meet Wayne, one of Ellen's co-workers, who had been with the company about as long as Ellen when the changes came along.

Wayne saw his division consolidated with another part of the company. Like Ellen, he had to say good-bye to a number of close friends.

Like Ellen, Wayne was asked to assume new responsibilities, including researching areas of the company's business which were unfamiliar to him. He was also asked to help retrain some of the firm's workers.

Although he got to keep his old office, Wayne found out that, as a cost-cutting measure, he would have to do without a secretary on certain days of the week.

And, like Ellen, Wayne had to face mastering new computer technology, including lap-top models.

CHOOSE to CHANGE

Unlike Ellen, though, Wayne **CHOSE** to view each change in his company as a **NEGATIVE DISCOVERY.** When he learned that Tom, a long-time friend in the accounting department, was being transferred out of state, he took no ACTION. He did not say good-bye to Tom. As a result, Wayne *lost* **ENERGY,** and *felt* **WORSE** instead of BETTER.

Wayne did not make an effort to introduce himself to the company's new workers, and even passed up an opportunity to attend a "Welcome New Employees" party organized by Ellen and some other company veterans. Presented with an easy opportunity to **TAKE ACTION,** Wayne **CHOSE to do nothing, and felt even WORSE.**

With the same workload, yet less secretarial assistance, Wayne again took **no ACTION.** He maintained his one-hour lunch, and began eating more fattening foods he thought would make him feel BETTER. His work began to pile up, making him **feel much WORSE,** since he had always prided himself on being an efficient worker. At this point Wayne had lost so much ENERGY that he began to experience distress. He even felt sharp stomach pains from time to time.

YOU CAN make CHANGES in your life POSITIVE if you CHOOSE to

In sharp contrast to workers like Ellen, Wayne paid little attention to the new computer technology offered by the company. He left the manuals unopened on his desk, and continued to rely on the old machines -- even though he knew they would be phased out within a few months.

Sitting alone in his office most of the day, Wayne looked forlornly at the piles of work he had not touched, including the unopened computer manuals -- and started to *feel WORSE* and *WORSE* and *WORSE*. Some days he felt TERRIBLE -- almost without any ENERGY at all. Everywhere he looked while at his job he saw *NEGATIVE DISCOVERY*.

In one case, though, Wayne did *TAKE ACTION*. But it wasn't really positive, con-structive, or appropriate. Faced with the immi-nent prospect of having to retrain some of the company's workers, to teach them new skills, Wayne went to his supervisor and asked to be relieved of this new responsibility.

CHANGE is essentially neutral
YOU make it POSITIVE
or NEGATIVE by YOUR RESPONSE

It wasn't that he disliked the new workers, he told Jane, his boss. It was just that he felt uncomfortable doing something this different -- after all, he'd never done any formal teaching before. Even when Jane suggested that he at least give the retraining a try for a week or so, Wayne insisted on saying no.

For a day or two after this, Wayne felt a little **BETTER**. He told himself that work felt a little like the old days. He even thought of calling Tom to see how things were going.

But Wayne's work continued to pile up, and the clock seemed to go slower every day. At this point, Wayne's distress progressed into illness. He started to have trouble sleeping, and woke up in the middle of the night a lot. He put on ten pounds, and stopped taking walks every other day like he'd done for years. Most mornings he wondered how he'd find the ENERGY to go to work.

Finally, his wife convinced him to go for his annual physical three months early. The doctor quickly noted Wayne's stress symptoms, and told him that his blood pressure had risen alarmingly. Wayne admitted that work had been bothering him for some time, and explained briefly.

CHANGE

The doctor suggested that Wayne visit an occupational counselor his company was making available to workers who, like Wayne, were having trouble adjusting to the many changes occurring in the workplace. The first few visits would even be paid for by the company.

Would Wayne *TAKE ACTION* at this point -- ACTION which would help him feel BETTER and start to restore the ENERGY needed to function efficiently at work?

Hopefully.

But only if Wayne could break the cycle of *CHOOSING* to view each of the work-related changes in his life as *NEGATIVE DISCOVERIES* .

As this tale of two workers shows all of us, CHANGE in the workplace -- or anywhere in our lives, for that matter -- is essentially neutral. CHANGE is not always clearly POSITIVE or NEGATIVE. *Whether CHANGE turns into POSITIVE DISCOVERY or NEGATIVE DISCOVERY depends on how we CHOOSE to respond to each CHANGE.*

CHOOSE to view CHANGE as POSITIVE and you will FEEL BETTER

CHANGE is a reality in all of our lives -- at work, at home, in personal relationships. Those you *CHOOSE* to see as *POSITIVE DISCOVERIES* will give you *ENERGY,* and help you feel *BETTER -- GOOD -- TERRIFIC!!!* Changes you **CHOOSE** to make into *NEGATIVE DISCOVERIES* will reduce your ENERGY level. If you do not TAKE ACTION to help you feel BETTER, you will feel steadily worse, experiencing distress and eventually illness.

The CHOICE is yours!!!

The most common **NEGATIVE DISCOV-ERIES** we must deal with on a daily basis go by a very common name. We call them "problems".

How many problems do you face in the course of an average day -- 5, 10, 15, 20, 25, more? If you're normal you face a lot. Each one of these "little" problems is a NEGATIVE DISCOVERY -- a "hit" against your overall daily energy.

But no matter how many problems life sends you each day, you will feel *BETTER* if you *TAKE ACTION* every time you must confront a problem.

"PROBLEMS" -- reduce your energy

If the dog's sick,
>> *TAKE ACTION:*
>>> Call the vet.

If you're caught in a traffic jam,
>> *TAKE ACTION:*
>>> Turn on your radio.

If your son or daughter is having problems with a subject in school,
>> *TAKE ACTION:*
>>> Arrange to speak with the teacher.

If you have a fight with your spouse or companion,
>> *TAKE ACTION:*
>>> Arrange to talk it over.

If you disagree with your company's policies,
>> *TAKE ACTION:*
>>> Write a memo to the boss.

If someone at work criticizes you,
>> *TAKE ACTION:*
>>> Ask him or her to explain the problem.

ACTION
&
MORE ACTION

Will your dog be all right?
Maybe.

Will the traffic improve?
Possibly.

Will your child be a better student?
Hopefully.

Will your relationship with your spouse or companion improve?
It might happen.

Will your company change its policies?
Could be.

But you will feel **BETTER** -- no matter what the outcome -- because in every case you **TOOK ACTION** when you had a problem, when you were faced with a **NEGATIVE DISCOVERY**.

Let's be honest: *Feeling GOOD* is often very hard to accomplish -- especially in view of the many **NEGATIVE DISCOVERIES** we all encounter in life. You can't always achieve feeling GOOD or TERRIFIC.

Feeling GOOD is often hard
Feeling BETTER is much easier

But you can always feel *BETTER*.

And if you can get into the habit of feeling *BETTER*, you'll feel GOOD much of the time and TERRIFIC a good deal of the time.

But you must *TAKE ACTION*.

Why?

Because *indecision* -- just thinking about taking action -- costs ENERGY. When you're in a state of indecision, you lose ENERGY.

Making a decision will automatically cause you to feel *BETTER*. Even if you don't know if your decision is the correct one, *TAKING ACTION* will create *ENERGY* in your body and you will feel *BETTER*.

Even choosing between two extremely unpleasant alternatives will result in ENERGY. Cancer patients who finally choose a course of treatment -- even when they know that the course of treatment they've chosen will entail discomfort -- feel *BETTER*. They certainly don't feel GOOD or TERRIFIC, but they do feel *BETTER*, because they made a decision.

Indecision costs us ENERGY

You have to be careful, though -- it's not enough to just decide.

Consider this story:

Three frogs were sitting on a lily pad.

One frog decided to jump in.

How many frogs were left on the lily pad?
       Two?

Try again.
       One?

Nope.

The answer: THREE!!!

Why?

Because the "daring" frog only DECIDED to jump in. He didn't TAKE ACTION.

You must *TAKE ACTION* not only to counteract negative "hits" in life, but also to keep yourself on a personal growth pattern that's exhilarating.

Remember this equation:

$$K + A = B\ B$$

What's it mean?

KNOWLEDGE + ACTION = BIG BENEFITS

You know what will make you feel *BETTER*. All you have to do is *ACT* on that knowledge to receive *BIG BENEFITS*.

So when life hits you with *NEGATIVE DISCOVERY* -- big or small -- use your *KNOWLEDGE* to **TAKE ACTION** and enjoy *BIG BENEFITS*: feeling *BETTER* -- *GOOD* -- *TERRIFIC*.

*KNOWLEDGE
plus ACTION
equals BIG BENEFITS*

Sometime when life hits you with a huge *NEGATIVE DISCOVERY*, and you feel you just can't TAKE ACTION, and your ENERGY is so low you've given up on *BETTER -- GOOD -- TERRIFIC*, I want you to think about this story.

A man approached me after a conference one day and said that my ideas had helped him to feel *BETTER*. We talked for awhile and I asked him to share his story with me.

This is what he told me.

MICKEY'S STORY

He and his wife have two children. One child is eight years old and perfectly healthy.

The other child is five and a half, and his name is Mickey. Since his birth, Mickey has had to have five open-heart surgeries.

Each time the doctors had said that Mickey had less than a two percent chance to survive, because the operation is that serious.

But each time, some way, somehow, Mickey found a way to survive. The doctors don't understand it, but they say the kid has a strong will to live. And, some way, somehow, he pulls through.

So I asked the father, "What is Mickey's problem?"

He went on to say that Mickey needed a heart-lung transplant, and that if Mickey was to walk any short distance he would get very, very tired because his body cannot transfer oxygen to the blood adequately.

The man said that on one particular occasion a phone call came to the home. His wife got the call, and after the call his wife started to cry profusely.

Mickey happened to be there and he watched his mother crying on the phone.

Then she walked upstairs to the second floor of their home, went in their bedroom and continued to cry.

Some way, somehow, Mickey made his way up the stairs into his mother's bedroom -- which by itself was almost a miracle because of his condition.

Yet he made it into his mother's room, where she continued to cry, and he said, "Mom, what's wrong?"

And so his mother composed herself a little bit and she said, "Well, that was the doctor and the doctor said they still haven't found a way to correct your condition, but they're going to continue to work on it until they find a way to do what they have to do to help correct your condition."

And then she continued to cry a little bit.

Mickey looked at his mother and said, **"Mom, I have two good eyes, two good ears, one good nose, I can still smile, and that's not so bad."**

Mickey has had five open-heart surgeries. Mickey has had a lot of pain.

The prognosis for Mickey may not be all that bright, and yet this little boy can still see what he's got going for himself.

He can still recognize what's GOOD in his life, and he can still guide his mother and his father and the physicians around him and say, "Hey, I'm willing to move on. I still have a chance. I still have hope. And that's not so bad."

In the midst of a horrible series of **NEGATIVE DISCOVERIES**, this young boy was still able to **TAKE ACTION** and make things **BETTER** for himself and the people around him.

Hopefully, none of you will ever be as far down as Mickey in life. Hopefully, **NEGATIVE DISCOVERY** will never knock you down this far.

But whatever **NEGATIVE DISCOVERIES** come your way in life, no matter how BAD things get, you can still take **ACTION** and feel **BETTER**, and hopefully work your way back to feeling **BETTER -- GOOD -- TERRIFIC.**

Don't allow NEGATIVE DISCOVERY
to overwhelm you --
TAKE ACTION

Summary

NEGATIVE DISCOVERY is part of life.

Life gives us both good and bad surprises.

While *POSITIVE DISCOVERY* increases our overall level of energy, *NEGATIVE DISCOVERY* -- no matter how small or large -- costs us ENERGY.

When life surprises you with a NEGATIVE DISCOVERY, *TAKE ACTION* which is appropriate, positive, and constructive. This *ACTION* will not make you feel GOOD or TERRIFIC, but you will *feel* *BETTER*.

NEGATIVE DISCOVERY not confronted by ACTION can lead to distress. If the distress continues, you may suffer disease.

ACTION is the key.

If you always *TAKE ACTION* when you must deal with NEGATIVE DISCOVERY, you will feel *BETTER*. You will raise your ENERGY level as a result, and be on your way to once again feeling *BETTER -- GOOD -- TERRIFIC.*

Deciding isn't good enough. You must *ACT*. NEGATIVE DISCOVERY is real. No matter how you deal with it, it reduces your system's overall ENERGY.

So get into the habit: Every time NEGATIVE DISCOVERY "hits", *TAKE ACTION* as soon as possible. If you do this every time NEGATIVE DISCOVERY comes your way, you'll feel *BETTER* faster, and be back on your way to feeling

BETTER!

GOOD!!

TERRIFIC!!!

Now let's put what you've learned about NEGATIVE DISCOVERY to work.

For the next thirty days, chart the *NEGATIVE DISCOVERIES* which occur in your life --and the *ACTION* you took to deal with each of them. Don't leave out the small ones -- use extra sheets of paper if necessary.

In the first column, briefly describe each NEGATIVE DISCOVERY.

Use the second column to say what *ACTION* you took to reduce the "hit" against your ENERGY by the NEGATIVE DISCOVERY.

Finally, use the number continuum to the right to show how much **BETTER** you felt after *TAKING ACTION* following each NEGATIVE DISCOVERY.

If you're developing a pattern of *TAKING ACTION* -- positive, constructive, appropriate ACTION every time NEGATIVE DISCOVERY "hits" in your life -- you might see something like this by Day 30 on the next page.

Develop a pattern of
TAKING ACTION
after each
NEGATIVE DISCOVERY

NEGATIVE DISCOVERY LOG (exhibit C)

Day #30   Date: _____

NEGATIVE DISCOVERY	ACTION (How did you help it happen?)	HOW DID IT MAKE YOU FEEL?
1. Kitchen sink piled sky high with dirty dishes	Did one small load before going to bed	1 2 ③ 4 5 6 7 8 9 10 (circle one)
2. Mechanic called -- $100 car repair is now $500	Called car dealer to discuss why this problem developed	1 ② 3 4 5 6 7 8 9 10 (circle one)
3. Clients report difficulty in reaching me at work	Called boss to discuss new company phone system	1 2 3 ④ 5 6 7 8 9 10 (circle one)
4. Spouse complained that we don't have time together	Discussed possibility of taking more trips with spouse	1 2 3 4 5 6 ⑦ 8 9 10 (circle one)
5. Due to small tax refund couldn't afford Hawaii trip	Talked to travel agent, who suggested Caribbean alternative	1 2 3 4 5 6 7 8 ⑨ 10 (circle one)

NEGATIVE DISCOVERY LOG (exhibit D)

Day # 1

Date: _____

NEGATIVE DISCOVERY	ACTION (How did you help it happen?)	HOW DID IT MAKE YOU FEEL? BETTER-GOOD-TERRIFIC
1. _____	_____	1 2 3 4 5 6 7 8 9 10 (circle one)
2. _____	_____	1 2 3 4 5 6 7 8 9 10 (circle one)
3. _____	_____	1 2 3 4 5 6 7 8 9 10 (circle one)
4. _____	_____	1 2 3 4 5 6 7 8 9 10 (circle one)
5. _____	_____	1 2 3 4 5 6 7 8 9 10 (circle one)

NEGATIVE DISCOVERY LOG (exhibit D)

Day # 2

Date: _____

NEGATIVE DISCOVERY	ACTION (How did you help it happen?)	HOW DID IT MAKE YOU FEEL? *BETTER-GOOD-TERRIFIC*
1. _____	_____	1 2 3 4 5 6 7 8 9 10 (circle one)
2. _____	_____	1 2 3 4 5 6 7 8 9 10 (circle one)
3. _____	_____	1 2 3 4 5 6 7 8 9 10 (circle one)
4. _____	_____	1 2 3 4 5 6 7 8 9 10 (circle one)
5. _____	_____	1 2 3 4 5 6 7 8 9 10 (circle one)

NEGATIVE DISCOVERY LOG (exhibit D)

Day # 3

Date: _____

NEGATIVE DISCOVERY	ACTION (How did you help it happen?)	HOW DID IT MAKE YOU FEEL? BETTER-GOOD-TERRIFIC
1.	_____ _____	1 2 3 4 5 6 7 8 9 10 (circle one)
2.	_____ _____	1 2 3 4 5 6 7 8 9 10 (circle one)
3.	_____ _____	1 2 3 4 5 6 7 8 9 10 (circle one)
4.	_____ _____	1 2 3 4 5 6 7 8 9 10 (circle one)
5.	_____ _____	1 2 3 4 5 6 7 8 9 10 (circle one)

NEGATIVE DISCOVERY LOG (exhibit D)

Date: _____

NEGATIVE DISCOVERY	ACTION (How did you help it happen?)	HOW DID IT MAKE YOU FEEL? *BETTER-GOOD-TERRIFIC*
1. _____	_____	1 2 3 4 5 6 7 8 9 10 (circle one)
2. _____	_____	1 2 3 4 5 6 7 8 9 10 (circle one)
3. _____	_____	1 2 3 4 5 6 7 8 9 10 (circle one)
4. _____	_____	1 2 3 4 5 6 7 8 9 10 (circle one)
5. _____	_____	1 2 3 4 5 6 7 8 9 10 (circle one)

NEGATIVE DISCOVERY LOG (exhibit D)

Day # **5**

Date: _____

NEGATIVE DISCOVERY	ACTION (How did you help it happen?)	HOW DID IT MAKE YOU FEEL? *BETTER-GOOD-TERRIFIC*
1. _____	_____	1 2 3 4 5 6 7 8 9 10 (circle one)
2. _____	_____	1 2 3 4 5 6 7 8 9 10 (circle one)
3. _____	_____	1 2 3 4 5 6 7 8 9 10 (circle one)
4. _____	_____	1 2 3 4 5 6 7 8 9 10 (circle one)
5. _____	_____	1 2 3 4 5 6 7 8 9 10 (circle one)

NEGATIVE DISCOVERY LOG (exhibit D)

Day # 6   Date: _____

NEGATIVE DISCOVERY	ACTION (How did you help it happen?)	HOW DID IT MAKE YOU FEEL? *BETTER-GOOD-TERRIFIC*
1. _____	_____	1 2 3 4 5 6 7 8 9 10 (circle one)
2. _____	_____	1 2 3 4 5 6 7 8 9 10 (circle one)
3. _____	_____	1 2 3 4 5 6 7 8 9 10 (circle one)
4. _____	_____	1 2 3 4 5 6 7 8 9 10 (circle one)
5. _____	_____	1 2 3 4 5 6 7 8 9 10 (circle one)

Day # 7

NEGATIVE DISCOVERY LOG (exhibit D)

Date: _____

NEGATIVE DISCOVERY	ACTION (How did you help it happen?)	HOW DID IT MAKE YOU FEEL? BETTER-GOOD-TERRIFIC
1. _____	_____	1 2 3 4 5 6 7 8 9 10 (circle one)
2. _____	_____	1 2 3 4 5 6 7 8 9 10 (circle one)
3. _____	_____	1 2 3 4 5 6 7 8 9 10 (circle one)
4. _____	_____	1 2 3 4 5 6 7 8 9 10 (circle one)
5. _____	_____	1 2 3 4 5 6 7 8 9 10 (circle one)

NEGATIVE DISCOVERY LOG (exhibit D)

Date: _____

Day # 8

NEGATIVE DISCOVERY	ACTION (How did you help it happen?)	HOW DID IT MAKE YOU FEEL? *BETTER-GOOD-TERRIFIC*
1. _____	_____	1 2 3 4 5 6 7 8 9 10 (circle one)
2. _____	_____	1 2 3 4 5 6 7 8 9 10 (circle one)
3. _____	_____	1 2 3 4 5 6 7 8 9 10 (circle one)
4. _____	_____	1 2 3 4 5 6 7 8 9 10 (circle one)
5. _____	_____	1 2 3 4 5 6 7 8 9 10 (circle one)

NEGATIVE DISCOVERY LOG (exhibit D)

Day # 9

Date: _____

NEGATIVE DISCOVERY	ACTION (How did you help it happen?)	HOW DID IT MAKE YOU FEEL? *BETTER-GOOD-TERRIFIC*
1. _____	_____	1 2 3 4 5 6 7 8 9 10 (circle one)
2. _____	_____	1 2 3 4 5 6 7 8 9 10 (circle one)
3. _____	_____	1 2 3 4 5 6 7 8 9 10 (circle one)
4. _____	_____	1 2 3 4 5 6 7 8 9 10 (circle one)
5. _____	_____	1 2 3 4 5 6 7 8 9 10 (circle one)

NEGATIVE DISCOVERY LOG (exhibit D)

Day # 1 0   Date: _____

NEGATIVE DISCOVERY	ACTION	HOW DID IT MAKE YOU FEEL?
	(How did you help it happen?)	BETTER-GOOD-TERRIFIC
1. _____	_____	1 2 3 4 5 6 7 8 9 10
		(circle one)
2. _____	_____	1 2 3 4 5 6 7 8 9 10
		(circle one)
3. _____	_____	1 2 3 4 5 6 7 8 9 10
		(circle one)
4. _____	_____	1 2 3 4 5 6 7 8 9 10
		(circle one)
5. _____	_____	1 2 3 4 5 6 7 8 9 10
		(circle one)

Day # 11

NEGATIVE DISCOVERY LOG (exhibit D)

Date: _____

NEGATIVE DISCOVERY	ACTION (How did you help it happen?)	HOW DID IT MAKE YOU FEEL? *BETTER-GOOD-TERRIFIC*
1. _____	_____ _____	1 2 3 4 5 6 7 8 9 10 (circle one)
2. _____	_____ _____	1 2 3 4 5 6 7 8 9 10 (circle one)
3. _____	_____ _____	1 2 3 4 5 6 7 8 9 10 (circle one)
4. _____	_____ _____	1 2 3 4 5 6 7 8 9 10 (circle one)
5. _____	_____ _____	1 2 3 4 5 6 7 8 9 10 (circle one)

NEGATIVE DISCOVERY LOG (exhibit D)

Day # 1 2   Date: _____

NEGATIVE DISCOVERY	ACTION (How did you help it happen?)	HOW DID IT MAKE YOU FEEL? *BETTER-GOOD-TERRIFIC*
1. _____	_____	1 2 3 4 5 6 7 8 9 10 (circle one)
2. _____	_____	1 2 3 4 5 6 7 8 9 10 (circle one)
3. _____	_____	1 2 3 4 5 6 7 8 9 10 (circle one)
4. _____	_____	1 2 3 4 5 6 7 8 9 10 (circle one)
5. _____	_____	1 2 3 4 5 6 7 8 9 10 (circle one)

NEGATIVE DISCOVERY LOG (exhibit D)

Day # 13

Date: _____

NEGATIVE DISCOVERY	ACTION (How did you help it happen?)	HOW DID IT MAKE YOU FEEL? *BETTER-GOOD-TERRIFIC*
1. _____	_____	1 2 3 4 5 6 7 8 9 10 (circle one)
2. _____	_____	1 2 3 4 5 6 7 8 9 10 (circle one)
3. _____	_____	1 2 3 4 5 6 7 8 9 10 (circle one)
4. _____	_____	1 2 3 4 5 6 7 8 9 10 (circle one)
5. _____	_____	1 2 3 4 5 6 7 8 9 10 (circle one)

NEGATIVE DISCOVERY LOG (exhibit D)

Day # 1 4   Date: _____

NEGATIVE DISCOVERY	ACTION (How did you help it happen?)	HOW DID IT MAKE YOU FEEL? *BETTER-GOOD-TERRIFIC*
1. _____	_____	1 2 3 4 5 6 7 8 9 10 (circle one)
2. _____	_____	1 2 3 4 5 6 7 8 9 10 (circle one)
3. _____	_____	1 2 3 4 5 6 7 8 9 10 (circle one)
4. _____	_____	1 2 3 4 5 6 7 8 9 10 (circle one)
5. _____	_____	1 2 3 4 5 6 7 8 9 10 (circle one)

NEGATIVE DISCOVERY LOG (exhibit D)

Day #15

Date: _____

NEGATIVE DISCOVERY	ACTION (How did you help it happen?)	HOW DID IT MAKE YOU FEEL? *BETTER-GOOD-TERRIFIC*
1. _____	_____	1 2 3 4 5 6 7 8 9 10 (circle one)
2. _____	_____	1 2 3 4 5 6 7 8 9 10 (circle one)
3. _____	_____	1 2 3 4 5 6 7 8 9 10 (circle one)
4. _____	_____	1 2 3 4 5 6 7 8 9 10 (circle one)
5. _____	_____	1 2 3 4 5 6 7 8 9 10 (circle one)

NEGATIVE DISCOVERY LOG (exhibit D)

Date: _____

Day # 1 6

NEGATIVE DISCOVERY	ACTION (How did you help it happen?)	HOW DID IT MAKE YOU FEEL? *BETTER-GOOD-TERRIFIC*
1. _____	_____ _____	1 2 3 4 5 6 7 8 9 10 (circle one)
2. _____	_____ _____	1 2 3 4 5 6 7 8 9 10 (circle one)
3. _____	_____ _____	1 2 3 4 5 6 7 8 9 10 (circle one)
4. _____	_____ _____	1 2 3 4 5 6 7 8 9 10 (circle one)
5. _____	_____ _____	1 2 3 4 5 6 7 8 9 10 (circle one)

Day # 17

NEGATIVE DISCOVERY LOG (exhibit D)

Date: _____

NEGATIVE DISCOVERY	ACTION (How did you help it happen?)	HOW DID IT MAKE YOU FEEL? *BETTER-GOOD-TERRIFIC*
1. _____	_____	1 2 3 4 5 6 7 8 9 10 (circle one)
2. _____	_____	1 2 3 4 5 6 7 8 9 10 (circle one)
3. _____	_____	1 2 3 4 5 6 7 8 9 10 (circle one)
4. _____	_____	1 2 3 4 5 6 7 8 9 10 (circle one)
5. _____	_____	1 2 3 4 5 6 7 8 9 10 (circle one)

NEGATIVE DISCOVERY LOG (exhibit D)

Day # 1 8   Date: _____

NEGATIVE DISCOVERY

ACTION
(How did you help it happen?)

HOW DID IT MAKE
YOU FEEL?
BETTER-GOOD-TERRIFIC

1. _____ _____ 1 2 3 4 5 6 7 8 9 10
                                                (circle one)

2. _____ _____ 1 2 3 4 5 6 7 8 9 10
                                                (circle one)

3. _____ _____ 1 2 3 4 5 6 7 8 9 10
                                                (circle one)

4. _____ _____ 1 2 3 4 5 6 7 8 9 10
                                                (circle one)

5. _____ _____ 1 2 3 4 5 6 7 8 9 10
                                                (circle one)

NEGATIVE DISCOVERY LOG (exhibit D)

Day # 19

Date: _____

NEGATIVE DISCOVERY	ACTION (How did you help it happen?)	HOW DID IT MAKE YOU FEEL? *BETTER-GOOD-TERRIFIC*
1. _____	_____	1 2 3 4 5 6 7 8 9 10 (circle one)
2. _____	_____	1 2 3 4 5 6 7 8 9 10 (circle one)
3. _____	_____	1 2 3 4 5 6 7 8 9 10 (circle one)
4. _____	_____	1 2 3 4 5 6 7 8 9 10 (circle one)
5. _____	_____	1 2 3 4 5 6 7 8 9 10 (circle one)

NEGATIVE DISCOVERY LOG (exhibit D)

Day # 20

Date: _____

NEGATIVE DISCOVERY	ACTION (How did you help it happen?)	HOW DID IT MAKE YOU FEEL? *BETTER-GOOD-TERRIFIC*
1. _____	_____	1 2 3 4 5 6 7 8 9 10 (circle one)
2. _____	_____	1 2 3 4 5 6 7 8 9 10 (circle one)
3. _____	_____	1 2 3 4 5 6 7 8 9 10 (circle one)
4. _____	_____	1 2 3 4 5 6 7 8 9 10 (circle one)
5. _____	_____	1 2 3 4 5 6 7 8 9 10 (circle one)

NEGATIVE DISCOVERY LOG (exhibit D)

Day # 2 1

Date: _____

NEGATIVE DISCOVERY	ACTION (How did you help it happen?)	HOW DID IT MAKE YOU FEEL? *BETTER-GOOD-TERRIFIC*
1. _____	_____	1 2 3 4 5 6 7 8 9 10 (circle one)
2. _____	_____	1 2 3 4 5 6 7 8 9 10 (circle one)
3. _____	_____	1 2 3 4 5 6 7 8 9 10 (circle one)
4. _____	_____	1 2 3 4 5 6 7 8 9 10 (circle one)
5. _____	_____	1 2 3 4 5 6 7 8 9 10 (circle one)

Day # 22

NEGATIVE DISCOVERY LOG (exhibit D)

Date: _____

NEGATIVE DISCOVERY	ACTION (How did you help it happen?)	HOW DID IT MAKE YOU FEEL? BETTER-GOOD-TERRIFIC
1. _____	_____	1 2 3 4 5 6 7 8 9 10 (circle one)
2. _____	_____	1 2 3 4 5 6 7 8 9 10 (circle one)
3. _____	_____	1 2 3 4 5 6 7 8 9 10 (circle one)
4. _____	_____	1 2 3 4 5 6 7 8 9 10 (circle one)
5. _____	_____	1 2 3 4 5 6 7 8 9 10 (circle one)

NEGATIVE DISCOVERY LOG (exhibit D)

Day # 23

Date: _____

NEGATIVE DISCOVERY	ACTION (How did you help it happen?)	HOW DID IT MAKE YOU FEEL? *BETTER-GOOD-TERRIFIC*
1. _____	_____	1 2 3 4 5 6 7 8 9 10 (circle one)
2. _____	_____	1 2 3 4 5 6 7 8 9 10 (circle one)
3. _____	_____	1 2 3 4 5 6 7 8 9 10 (circle one)
4. _____	_____	1 2 3 4 5 6 7 8 9 10 (circle one)
5. _____	_____	1 2 3 4 5 6 7 8 9 10 (circle one)

NEGATIVE DISCOVERY LOG (exhibit D)

Day # 2 4

Date: _____

NEGATIVE DISCOVERY	ACTION (How did you help it happen?)	HOW DID IT MAKE YOU FEEL? *BETTER-GOOD-TERRIFIC*
1. _____	_____	1 2 3 4 5 6 7 8 9 10 (circle one)
2. _____	_____	1 2 3 4 5 6 7 8 9 10 (circle one)
3. _____	_____	1 2 3 4 5 6 7 8 9 10 (circle one)
4. _____	_____	1 2 3 4 5 6 7 8 9 10 (circle one)
5. _____	_____	1 2 3 4 5 6 7 8 9 10 (circle one)

Day # 25

NEGATIVE DISCOVERY LOG (exhibit D)

Date: _____

NEGATIVE DISCOVERY	ACTION (How did you help it happen?)	HOW DID IT MAKE YOU FEEL? *BETTER-GOOD-TERRIFIC*
1. _____	_____ _____	1 2 3 4 5 6 7 8 9 10 (circle one)
2. _____	_____ _____	1 2 3 4 5 6 7 8 9 10 (circle one)
3. _____	_____ _____	1 2 3 4 5 6 7 8 9 10 (circle one)
4. _____	_____ _____	1 2 3 4 5 6 7 8 9 10 (circle one)
5. _____	_____ _____	1 2 3 4 5 6 7 8 9 10 (circle one)

NEGATIVE DISCOVERY LOG (exhibit D)

Day # 2 6   Date: _____

NEGATIVE DISCOVERY

ACTION

(How did you help it happen?)

**HOW DID IT MAKE
YOU FEEL?**
BETTER-GOOD-TERRIFIC

1. _____   _____   1 2 3 4 5 6 7 8 9 10
                                          (circle one)

2. _____   _____   1 2 3 4 5 6 7 8 9 10
                                          (circle one)

3. _____   _____   1 2 3 4 5 6 7 8 9 10
                                          (circle one)

4. _____   _____   1 2 3 4 5 6 7 8 9 10
                                          (circle one)

5. _____   _____   1 2 3 4 5 6 7 8 9 10
                                          (circle one)

NEGATIVE DISCOVERY LOG (exhibit D)

Day # 27

Date: _____

NEGATIVE DISCOVERY	ACTION (How did you help it happen?)	HOW DID IT MAKE YOU FEEL? BETTER-GOOD-TERRIFIC
1.		1 2 3 4 5 6 7 8 9 10 (circle one)
2.		1 2 3 4 5 6 7 8 9 10 (circle one)
3.		1 2 3 4 5 6 7 8 9 10 (circle one)
4.		1 2 3 4 5 6 7 8 9 10 (circle one)
5.		1 2 3 4 5 6 7 8 9 10 (circle one)

NEGATIVE DISCOVERY LOG (exhibit D)

Day # 2 8

Date: _____

NEGATIVE DISCOVERY	ACTION (How did you help it happen?)	HOW DID IT MAKE YOU FEEL? *BETTER-GOOD-TERRIFIC*
1. _____	_____	1 2 3 4 5 6 7 8 9 10 (circle one)
2. _____	_____	1 2 3 4 5 6 7 8 9 10 (circle one)
3. _____	_____	1 2 3 4 5 6 7 8 9 10 (circle one)
4. _____	_____	1 2 3 4 5 6 7 8 9 10 (circle one)
5. _____	_____	1 2 3 4 5 6 7 8 9 10 (circle one)

NEGATIVE DISCOVERY LOG (exhibit D)

Day # 2 9

Date: _____

NEGATIVE DISCOVERY	ACTION (How did you help it happen?)	HOW DID IT MAKE YOU FEEL? *BETTER-GOOD-TERRIFIC*
1. _____	_____	1 2 3 4 5 6 7 8 9 10 (circle one)
2. _____	_____	1 2 3 4 5 6 7 8 9 10 (circle one)
3. _____	_____	1 2 3 4 5 6 7 8 9 10 (circle one)
4. _____	_____	1 2 3 4 5 6 7 8 9 10 (circle one)
5. _____	_____	1 2 3 4 5 6 7 8 9 10 (circle one)

NEGATIVE DISCOVERY LOG (exhibit D)

Day # 3 0

Date: _____

NEGATIVE DISCOVERY	ACTION (How did you help it happen?)	HOW DID IT MAKE YOU FEEL? *BETTER-GOOD-TERRIFIC*
1. _____	_____	1 2 3 4 5 6 7 8 9 10 (circle one)
2. _____	_____	1 2 3 4 5 6 7 8 9 10 (circle one)
3. _____	_____	1 2 3 4 5 6 7 8 9 10 (circle one)
4. _____	_____	1 2 3 4 5 6 7 8 9 10 (circle one)
5. _____	_____	1 2 3 4 5 6 7 8 9 10 (circle one)

PART III

REVIEW:

START

DISCOVERING

TODAY!!!!

Each of us is a living human system. We need **ENERGY** -- not only to function, but also to grow. And we need this ENERGY every day of our lives to feel **BETTER -- GOOD -- TERRIFIC!!** One powerful source of ENERGY that anyone can tap into is **DISCOVERY.**

POSITIVE DISCOVERY happens in many ways -- when we learn, give, love, change. A POSITIVE DISCOVERY can be as small as seeing a beautiful flower or as big as winnning first place in the flower show. Whatever the size, POSITIVE DISCOVERY always creates ENERGY -- ENERGY which can help us feel **BETTER** every day.

POSITIVE DISCOVERIES come most often to people who are in DISCOVERY MODE -- people who take risks, look at life in new ways, make changes in their lives, and open their minds to new experiences.

DISCOVERY, though, can also be NEGATIVE. **NEGATIVE DISCOVERY** happens when we receive bad news, when we're hurt, when things don't go our way. Since NEGATIVE DISCOVERY lowers your level of ENERGY, you must **TAKE ACTION** each time a NEGATIVE DISCOVERY "hits".

It's important to understand both POSITIVE and NEGATIVE DISCOVERY

It will make you feel *BETTER* -- no matter how painful the NEGATIVE DISCOVERY. If you always *TAKE ACTION* every time a NEGATIVE DISCOVERY occurs, you'll develop a resilient ENERGY system. You'll bounce back faster, and be able to feel *BETTER -- GOOD -- TERRIFIC* more of the time.

For the next month -- start today -- make the magic of DISCOVERY more a part of your day-to-day living.

Take a few risks, try a few new things, make a few changes in your life, open your mind to the world around you. Try even the littlest things: wear a shirt or blouse you haven't had on for months, drive a different route home from work, watch a TV program on a channel you don't normally view, rearrange a room in your house, call an old friend. *Attempt at least one different behavior each day which could create a POSITIVE DISCOVERY -- a sudden burst of ENERGY which will make you feel BETTER.*

Attempt at least one NEW BEHAVIOR each day for the next month

On the other hand, when NEGATIVE DISCOVERY "hits" you during the next month, **TAKE ACTION** every time -- and as soon as possible. Again, don't overlook the little things: if the tub's clogged, grab the plunger or call the plumber; if your car's making a funny noise, call the garage and make an appointment; if you notice your shoes are worn, replace or repair them; if your desk is starting to "pile up", throw a few things out or put them in a file -- don't worry about the whole mess, because if you just clean up some of it, you'll feel **BETTER**.

But don't play games with yourself. You know a problem when you see one in your life. So when NEGATIVE DISCOVERIES come along -- no matter how small -- **TAKE ACTION**. Don't just decide. Act. Do something positive, constructive, and appropriate right away.

Each day during the coming month jot down a few notes in the MONTHLY LOG about how you felt for most of that day. Ask yourself how much ENERGY you had during most of that day. Be honest. *Use the terms TERRIBLE -- BAD - - BETTER -- GOOD -- TERRIFIC if you want.*

Be HONEST
record your TRUE FEELINGS

The MONTHLY LOG will provide a summary of the charts you completed at the end of Part I (exhibit B pages 50-79) and Part II (exhibit D pages 113-142).

Use these number ratings to determine how you *felt* on each day.

1-2 - - TERRIBLE

3-4 - - BAD

5-6 - - BETTER!

7-8 - - GOOD!!

9-10 - - TERRIFIC!!!

It's how
you FEEL
that REALLY counts

MONTHLY LOG

DAY	NUMBER	COMMENTS
# 1	_____	_____
		_____
# 2	_____	_____
		_____
# 3	_____	_____
		_____
# 4	_____	_____
		_____
# 5	_____	_____
		_____
# 6	_____	_____
		_____
# 7	_____	_____
		_____

DAY	NUMBER	COMMENTS
#8	_____	_____
		_____
#9	_____	_____
		_____
#10	_____	_____
		_____
#11	_____	_____
		_____
#12	_____	_____
		_____
#13	_____	_____
		_____
#14	_____	_____
		_____
#15	_____	_____
		_____

DAY NUMBER	COMMENTS
#16 _____	_____
	_____
#17 _____	_____
	_____
#18 _____	_____
	_____
#19 _____	_____
	_____
#20 _____	_____
	_____
#21 _____	_____
	_____
#22 _____	_____
	_____
#23 _____	_____
	_____

DAY NUMBER   **COMMENTS**

#24 _____   _____

                   _____

#25 _____   _____

                   _____

#26 _____   _____

                   _____

#27 _____   _____

                   _____

#28 _____   _____

                   _____

#29 _____   _____

                   _____

#30 _____   _____

                   _____

If you're discovering the magic in **DISCOVERY**, you'll see things get a lot better by the end of the month. If you've created opportunities for POSITIVE DISCOVERY to happen, if you **TOOK ACTION** every time you had a NEGATIVE DISCOVERY, you should have more ENERGY as the month progresses. You should be writing down **"BETTER"** frequently, "GOOD" a lot, and even "TERRIFIC" from time to time.

If you're also using the numbering system described above, you should see the numbers steadily get higher and higher.

It has to happen. Because the magic of DISCOVERY gives you ENERGY -- ENERGY which will make you feel **BETTER**.

And feeling **BETTER** is what we all want.

I hope this book has made you feel **BETTER**, and that you will work to harness the ENERGY OF DISCOVERY during the next month -- and far, far beyond.

The magic of DISCOVERY gives you ENERGY every time

Use **DISCOVERY** to give you more and more
ENERGY -- ENERGY which will propel you to
achieve a consistently HIGH-ENERGY LIFE.

So that you will feel

BETTER!

GOOD!

TERRIFIC!!!

But . . .

Remember the Introduction?

Continue to DISCOVER every day until you DISCOVER what it is you REALLY want to do with your life!

What it is that you've always wanted to do.

What it is that will not only *ENERGIZE* you but *EXCITE* you every day for the rest of your life.

That's the *ultimate DISCOVERY* -- for you, for those close to you.

Make that *DISCOVERY* and you will truly have found that

There's MAGIC in DISCOVERY!!!

ABOUT THE AUTHOR

John J. Pelizza, Ph.D., is:

A leading authority on wellness, change process, motivation and stress management

A professor of Health Education, and former Chairman of the Department of Health Education, The Sage Colleges, Troy, New York

The Consulting Director of the Wellness Center and Management Team, St. Clare's Hospital, Schenectady, New York

A dynamic speaker to over one hundred business, professional, and civic groups throughout the United States

The author of <u>Foot in the Door</u>, a book on managing stress in your personal and professional life

The author of <u>Thoughts to Make You THINK and FEEL BETTER,</u> a collection of inspirational quotes to make you think and feel better

The producer of an audio cassette, "Staying Motivated During Change", which deals with motivation and change in everyday life

The producer of an audio cassette tape, "Keys to High Energy Living" which discusses the principles of Discovery, Action, Growth and Closure

The creator and presenter of PPP, "Pelizza's Positive Principles", which airs weekly on WPTR AM 1540, Schenectady, New York

The creator of "Pelizza's Principles for Positive Living," a newsletter about wellness, stress management, and personal growth

A winner of the "Outstanding Young Alumni Award" from Pittsburg State University, Pittsburg, Kansas

A former President of the New York State Public Health Association, Northeastern Region

The developer of a specialized Self-Power Concepts Program for Vietnam Veterans and their spouses

A contributor of articles to professional journals and health education text-books

The founder of Pelizza & Associates, an organization devoted to helping people attain personal growth and wellness -- to helping people feel BETTER and do BETTER

Personal Growth Materials Available from Pelizza & Associates

AUDIO TAPES

"Keys to High Energy Living"

Dr. Pelizza illustrates several key principles which can increase the ENERGY you need to feel BETTER and do BETTER. He discusses the Principles of DISCOVERY, ACTION, GROWTH, and CLOSURE -- all of which, when applied in daily life, will enable you to live at a consistently higher level of ENERGY -- to feel BETTER and accomplish more every day.

"Staying Motivated During Change"

This tape demonstrates what MOTIVATION is. How to create it in your life every day. How to MOTIVATE yourself and how to MOTIVATE others. You'll also learn to respond to CHANGE in ways that will ENERGIZE you instead of depress you.

Especially recommended for workers who need to respond POSITIVELY to changes in their professional life.

BOOKS

"Foot in the Door"

Learn SELF-POWER CONCEPTS to lead a more POSITIVE and PRODUCTIVE life. SELF-POWER CONCEPTS refers to a body of knowledge about your own capacity to grow -- to be in control of your life, to think POSITIVELY and effectively, to set life goals, to manage stress, to benefit from failure, and to develop a personal affirmation program for yourself.

Features areas for listing your Life Goals and Action Plans. There is also a personal diary section for personal and professional growth.

"Thoughts to Make you THINK . . . and FEEL BETTER"

A collection of inspirational sayings, thoughts, and simple concepts about feeling BETTER and doing BETTER -- every day. You'll receive "food for thought" on a variety of topics, including change, choice, achievement, discipline, growth, and feeling BETTER!

Throughout the book there are twelve questions that help the reader identify what they really want in life.

This book makes an excellent gift and features a "to and from" page allowing you to write a personal thought to someone on a special occasion.

"There's MAGIC in DISCOVERY!"

DISCOVER the ENERGY that can be yours every day of your life by harnessing the power of DISCOVERY.

Begin by learning to recognize POSITIVE DISCOVERY in your life. Find out how to put yourself into DISCOVERY MODE and enjoy one POSITIVE DISCOVERY after another -- more and more ENERGY to feel BETTER and do BETTER!

Learn also how to use the PRINCIPLE OF ACTION to manage NEGATIVE DISCOVERY. Find out what to do when bad things happen, when life "hits" you in ways that reduce your ENERGY. DISCOVER how to bounce back more quickly and recover the ENERGY you need to feel BETTER -- GOOD -- TERRIFIC every day!

Features charts to help you monitor your progress in gaining more and more ENERGY from DISCOVERY.

NEWSLETTER

Pelizza's Principles for Positive Living

A bimonthly newsletter designed to help you feel **BETTER** and do **BETTER** by managing your THINKING and taking ACTION.

Each issue includes an illustration of one of Dr. Pelizza's key principles for living more positively, stories from real life, letters and anecdotes from readers. There's even a recipe to help you eat **BETTER**!

"Principles for Positive Living" is also the best way to keep up with Pelizza & Associates' newest publications, programs, and seminars.

GUEST SPEAKER

Dr. Pelizza is available to speak to groups, organizations, businesses and companies. He can tailor programs to meet your individual needs.

The following topics may be of interest to you:

- There's MAGIC in DISCOVERY

- Stress Management for HIGH-ENERGY Living

- Staying Motivated during CHANGE

- Eight Habits for Mental Fitness

- BETTER Customer Service through Personal Growth

- The Common Link in Sales and Performance

WRITE TO: Pelizza & Associates
P.O. Box 225
North Chatham, N.Y. 12132
(518) 766-4849
    or call
The Sage Colleges
Department of Health Educaation
Troy, New York 12180
(518) 270-2357

NOTES

NOTES

NOTES

NOTES